Second-Grade Math
A Month-to-Month Guide

2

Second-Grade Math

A Month-to-Month Guide

2

Nancy Litton

Math Solutions Publications
Sausalito, CA

Math Solutions Publications
A division of
Marilyn Burns Education Associates
150 Gate 5 Road, Suite 101
Sausalito, CA 94965
www.mathsolutions.com

Library of Congress Cataloging-in-Publication Data
Litton, Nancy, 1947–
   Second-grade math : a month-to-month guide / Nancy Litton.
      p. cm.
Includes bibliographical references and index.
   ISBN 0-941355-55-1 (alk. paper)
   1. Mathematics—Study and teaching (Elementary)—United
States—Handbooks, manuals, etc. 2. Curriculum planning—United
States—Handbooks, manuals, etc. I. Title.
   QA135.6.L57 2003
   372.7—dc22
                                        2003015692

Editor: Toby Gordon
Production: Melissa L. Inglis
Cover and interior design: Catherine Hawkes/Cat and Mouse
Composition: Argosy Publishing

Printed in the United States of America on acid-free paper
07 06 05 04 03 ML 1 2 3 4 5

A Message from Marilyn Burns

We at Marilyn Burns Education Associates believe that teaching mathematics well calls for increasing our understanding of the math we teach, seeking greater insight into how children learn mathematics, and refining lessons to best promote children's learning. All of our Math Solutions Professional Development publications and inservice courses have been designed to help teachers achieve these goals.

Our publications include a wide range of choices, from books in our new Teaching Arithmetic and Lessons for Algebraic Thinking series to resources that link math and literacy; from books to help teachers understand mathematics more deeply to children's books that help students develop an appreciation for math while learning basic concepts.

Our inservice programs offer five-day courses, one-day workshops, and series of school-year sessions throughout the country, working in partnership with school districts to help implement and sustain long-term improvement in mathematics instruction in all classrooms.

To find a complete listing of our publications and workshops, please visit our Web site at *www.mathsolutions.com*. Or contact us by calling (800) 868-9092 or sending an e-mail to *info@mathsolutions.com*.

We're eager for your feedback and interested in learning about your particular needs. We look forward to hearing from you.

A DIVISION OF MARILYN BURNS EDUCATION ASSOCIATES

Contents

Contents

Foreword

One of the challenges of teaching mathematics is planning a coherent year of instruction. Not only must we address the important mathematics children need to learn, we also need to help children learn to think, reason, and become proficient problem solvers. And we also want to inspire children to enjoy mathematics and see it as useful to their lives. Accomplishing this is a tall order that calls for understanding the full scope of the mathematics curriculum, having a rich repertoire of instructional options, being skilled at managing instruction in the classroom, and understanding the needs of the individual students in your class.

This book offers a month-by-month guide for planning a year of math instruction. It is one of a three-book series, each written by a master teacher to address teaching mathematics in grades one, two, and three. The author of each book acknowledges that her suggestions do not comprise the only approach to accomplish planning, or necessarily the best approach for others to follow. Rather, each suggests a thoughtful, practical, and very personal approach to planning that has grown out of her years of experience in the classroom.

The three authors of this series are truly master teachers—experienced, caring, hard-working, and incredibly accomplished. They bring their wisdom and experience to their books in unique ways, but as teachers they share common experiences and outlooks. Each has offered many professional development classes and workshops for teachers while also choosing to make classroom teaching the main focus of their careers. For all three of them, mathematics was not their initial love or strength. However, they each came to study and learn to appreciate mathematics because of their need to serve their students. They are committed to excellence in math instruction, they understand children, they know how to manage classrooms, and they are passionate about teaching. It is a great pleasure to present these books to you.

MARILYN BURNS

Acknowledgments

This book contains much of what I've learned over the course of my thirty-plus-year career as a primary teacher. Since I gleaned most of that knowledge from others, I'd like to take this opportunity to thank those individuals who have contributed most directly to my thinking as a teacher of primary mathematics.

I've been extraordinarily fortunate in always having exemplary teaching colleagues in the classrooms next door to me. Gwyneth McMillan, my first mentor and later my teaching neighbor, taught me the importance of always starting with the children when planning *any* curriculum. When I worked with her as a kindergarten teacher in the late 1960s, I learned that defining sets and subsets was much less important than giving children real objects to count, sort, and build with. I didn't yet know what kinds of questions to ask to help children extend their learning, but I had a feeling that Gwen had put me on the right track.

Several years later, in the late 1970s and early 1980s, I had a chance to teach next to Roz Haberkern in an open-plan setting. Listening to her pose problems and ask questions of her second and third graders gave me a vision of what a really good mathematics program could look like. We shake our heads at the architectural folly of classrooms without walls, and yet I know how much I learned from watching Roz skillfully teach day in and day out. I understand completely when one of Roz's former students, now a graduate with a scientific degree that required advanced mathematics, says, "It was Mrs. Haberkern who taught me mathematics."

For many years, Suzanne Cotrufo and Lianne Morrison, my current colleagues, have shared and added to my vision of what is important for young learners. Most recently, their steadfastness in finding ways to avoid the ill effects of standardized testing on a developmentally appropriate curriculum has been invaluable. They've helped me maintain *my* standards. Those standards include what I learned initially from Gwyneth—that the children are most important—and that providing opportunities for deep understanding of concepts must always be my goal.

In addition to having great colleagues, I've also been fortunate to teach at a time when so many thoughtful resources for young children have been developed in the field of mathematics education. I had the good fortune to take a *Math Their Way* course from Mary Baratta-Lorton as a young kindergarten teacher. Before taking her course, I had the sense to know that I could never teach first graders math from a traditional textbook. But I had no idea what I might do if I decided to move up a grade. I think I was as excited about being introduced to the world of pattern as many of my young students have been in the ensuing years. Mary's book, *Mathematics Their Way*, made it possible for me to try a new grade level and gave me a glimpse of the breadth of mathematics.

Having a framework for thinking about the topic of number sense has been immensely helpful to me. Julie Contestable provided that framework in language that was simple and straightforward and filled with examples that relate to the mathematics that young children do. Julie has also served as a wonderful role model for teaching, whenever I've had the good luck to take a workshop from her.

Perhaps no one has been more influential or helpful to my mathematics teaching than Bonnie Tank. Her support has come from both the many resource books she has inspired and written, and the opportunities I've had to watch her teach. I'll never forget the day I observed her as she introduced one of her problem-solving lessons to a group of first graders. When one child started to lose focus, Bonnie gently put her arm around the child, bringing her back into the fold. Bonnie went on to give the children the clearest picture of what was expected in a voice that was warm, calm, and inviting. I watched the children eagerly engage with each other and with the problem, and said to myself, "That's just the kind of teacher I want to be!" I will never have Bonnie's creativity as a designer of lessons, but I hope I'll be able to use her lessons to engage children with that same level of kindness and clarity.

I also owe an enormous debt to Marilyn Burns. First, her leadership in the field of mathematics makes it easier for me to make the choices I make every day for my students. Her voice as a widely recognized educator provides legitimacy to a curriculum based on understanding, and supports me as I try new ideas in my classroom. And second, nothing has pushed me more to grow professionally than the opportunity to serve as a consultant in her summer inservice program. As an MBEA consultant, I've been introduced to a world inhabited by remarkable teachers and exciting ideas. I've been awestruck and terrified by what has been expected of me, but I am so appreciative of the opportunities I've been afforded.

And that brings me to Toby Gordon, who edited both this and the earlier book I wrote about communicating with parents. Toby first helped me define my subject and then provided encouragement and great suggestions as I struggled to get my ideas down on paper. The writing process has been long and sometimes downright painful, but it has helped me clarify and refine my thinking in a way that is very satisfying.

Thinking back on my own development as a teacher reminds me that change happens gradually and understanding develops over time. Years ago, when I student-taught in Gwyneth's classroom, she told me, "Nancy, you make mistakes, but you always learn from them. You're going to be just fine." I'm hoping this book might be a way to pass on those words of encouragement to all of you who are trying to stay open to new ideas. I want to give thanks to my many mentors, and also wish good luck to those of you who will be providing guidance to future generations of students.

Introduction

Several years ago, I had an experience that changed my personal and professional life. I was invited to participate in a project about second-grade math instruction—an invitation that included attending a monthly workshop that focused on a specific mathematical unit of study geared especially for second graders. During each workshop, I had the chance to become familiar with an instructional unit and I was encouraged to try out the activities back in my classroom. The workshops also included rich discussions about how children learn mathematics.

My professional life changed because participating in the project gave me the support I needed to present a math curriculum that was cohesive and developmentally appropriate. I learned how to surround my students with concepts, allowing them to develop understanding over time. The units matched my sense of what was right for children and added depth to the attempts I had already been making to help my students become confident, flexible problem solvers.

My personal life changed because I no longer had to spend every Sunday night anxiously trying to figure out what to do in the coming week with my students in mathematics. I no longer was plagued by such thoughts as, "Nancy, you're not prepared." "You feel uneasy because you don't really know if you're headed in the right direction." "You can't go to movies; you have to figure out what to do during math next week!"

My hope is that this book will give you some of the same support that I experienced through my participation in the second-grade project. I hope that it will make your teaching easier and less fraught with doubt as you go about the sometimes lonely job of crafting a year-long math program for your students. This book may also broaden your definition of what a problem-solving curriculum in mathematics can be, building on the assumption that students retain what they understand, and that they are most likely to understand concepts that are developed in a learning environment that provokes thinking and encourages interest and perseverance.

The book is meant as a general guide for yearlong planning, not as a blueprint to follow in a lockstep manner. The chapters follow the months of the school year and offer suggestions for topics to be covered from fall to spring. I've tried to provide a basic structure that will make you confident about your long-range planning and yet give you the freedom to make choices based on the needs and abilities of your students and on your own personal strengths and interests.

I hope this book also helps you with some of the minute-by-minute decision making that you face as a teacher. I've tried to figure out what makes lessons work for me so that I could suggest ways to help you support your students as they experience the pleasures and hard work associated with mathematical problem solving. Motivating and supporting students by presenting lessons well requires planning and understanding. Some of my suggestions may cause you to reflect on your teaching practices and give you the confidence to try new ideas in ways that feel right to you. Also, at the back of the book, you'll find a complete list of resources mentioned in the monthly chapters. I hope you'll turn to many of these curriculum guides to expand on the ideas presented in this book.

Learning math can be an intriguing and joyful experience for young learners. Number, shape, data collection, and measurement are all aspects of the world of mathematics that beckon to second graders' inquisitive minds. Exploring these ideas in the company of classmates who are excited about learning and who care about one another can establish positive attitudes about mathematics that will be important for years to come. I wish you the best of luck as you work with your students throughout the year.

Chapter 1

BEFORE THE CHILDREN ARRIVE

The week or two before the start of school is often full of both anticipation and anxiety. This time period can feel like a vacuum because you don't yet know your students. To be ready for the anticipated event, and to allay some anxiety, you can:

- prepare the classroom physically to receive children
- ground yourself in the basics of developing number sense in your students
- think through how you're going to schedule math each day
- give some thought to what your role will be as a teacher in a problem-solving-oriented math program ■

Setting Up the Mathematics Classroom

Preparing the classroom before the children's arrival has many benefits. It puts the room in order so that students have easy access to the materials and space they will need to be successful problem solvers. It can also help you settle into the new school year. The sense of order that you create is an important reminder that you are in charge and responsible for much of what goes on within the confines of your classroom. Teachers have many outside pressures—but when the students arrive and the classroom door is closed, you are in charge!

Manipulatives: The Basic Materials

Ideally, your classroom should be stocked with:

- Interlocking cubes can be used throughout the year for number work—gather at least 1 set of 1,000 cubes.
- Pattern blocks are extremely useful for geometry activities and draw children into mathematics with their bright colors and interrelated shapes—have at least 2 buckets of 250.
- Rulers, balance scales, and a clock with a second hand are necessary for measurement activities.
- Beans, bread tags, buttons, small ceramic tiles, color tiles, or any other small discrete material can be used as counters. These will provide variety and help your students understand that numeric concepts are not dependent on the size or shape of any one material.
- You'll need dice or cubes with the faces labeled 1 through 6 (and the corresponding number of dots on each face).
- You'll also want regular playing cards with the face cards removed. One deck of cards for every two students and a deck for yourself are needed.
- Geo blocks are nice for three-dimensional geometry activities.
- Multicolored, graduated-length Cuisenaire rods have an inherently mathematical nature. No formal lesson in this book requires Cuisenaire rods, but opportunities to build structures using the rods can help students explore important numeric relationships. They're a good material to have available during project time, which is described in the "Scheduling Math—Every Day" section of this chapter.

Making Materials Accessible

Place manipulative materials in containers (e.g., gallon plastic bags that you then store in a tub, or clear plastic boxes with stacking lids) in quan-

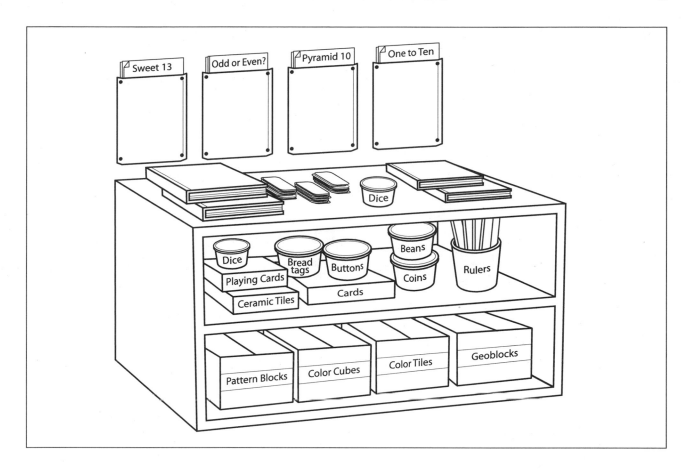

FIGURE 1–1   ▲

Making materials accessible to students.

tities adequate for a table of four students. Affix labels to the shelves indicating where each material is stored, to encourage students to be responsible for keeping the classroom organized.

If possible, store materials in low book shelves that are readily accessible to the children. Above the cabinet, tack large envelopes to hold copies of game/activity instructions. You can then use the shelf top to hold any unique materials needed for a specific game or activity. (See Figure 1–1.)

Room Arrangement

Rug Area

If possible, set aside an area of your room that is large enough for all of your students to sit around its perimeter. A chalkboard (or easel with a large pad of writing paper) should be visible to everyone. You'll use this arrangement when you want your students to listen to one another as they share their problem-solving strategies with the whole class. You'll also find this arrangement useful when you teach a new game or lead group discussions. The rug area creates a feeling of closeness that seems

FIGURE 1–2 ▶

A floor plan of partner seating.

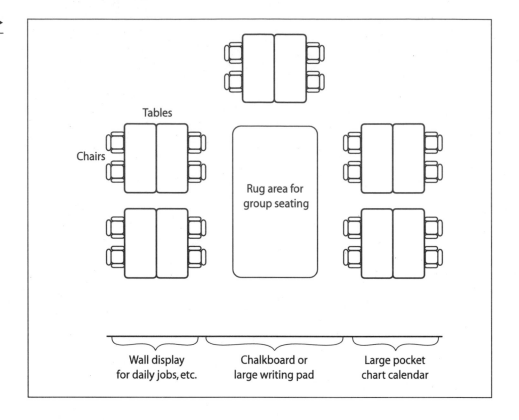

to help young children listen to one another, and it focuses their visual attention. It also gives them a break from sitting in the same chair all day long.

Partner Seating

Throughout the year, each student will often work with one other student, playing games or solving problems together. Rectangular tables that accommodate two students side by side are ideal. Also consider forming larger squares by pushing two tables together and then arranging these squares into a loose U-shape around the rug. With this arrangement, you have easy access to all students. Moreover, you can use this setting for those times when you want to conduct a group discussion with all the children at their tables. (See Figure 1–2.)

Wall Display for Daily Jobs

You may decide to have your students do the Daily Jobs described in Chapter 2. To be ready for the first day of school, set aside a large bulletin-board area, readily visible from both the children's seats and the rug area. In this area, you'll display calendar information, daily graphs and schedules, and a job chart. The wall display should include:

■ calendars—Use a monthly pocket-chart calendar (available commercially) that will be reorganized each month as the year progresses. Also post a commercial or small hand-made calendar for the current month (see Blackline Masters for one that may be enlarged). You'll use this calendar to post special days and to model crossing off each day as it passes by.

Sunday	Monday	Tuesday	Wednesday	Thursday	Friday	Saturday

■ pocket charts for today's date and number—Post the following frame sentences, written on sentence-strip paper, on a pocket chart:

Today is _____. (Have cards with the days of the week nearby on a long, narrow pocket chart.)

September XX, 200X. (Have cards with the months and the numbers 1–31 to rotate through these spaces.)

Today's Number is ___. (Have cards with the numbers 1–180, or higher if you have a longer school year. You'll also need a space elsewhere in the room to create a growing number line using these number cards.)

■ days-of-the-year chart—Include a large, blank grid, ten boxes across with as many rows as needed to provide one box for every day of the school year.

■ weather graph—Each month, post a new 8-by-11-inch graph with blank boxes next to the weather choices that are appropriate for your geographic area. (See Blackline Masters for a graph that may be enlarged.)

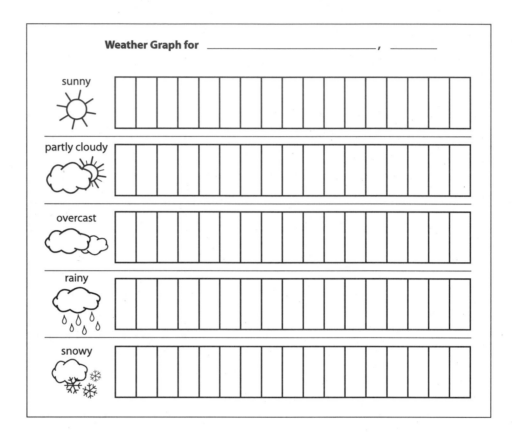

■ daily schedule—Write out the day's schedule with times on the chalkboard or on cards that fit in another pocket chart.

■ daily jobs chart—List the following four jobs and have a space for children's names to be rotated through the jobs: Today's Date, Weather Graph, Today's Number, Today's Calendar Page. (See Figure 1–3.)

Math Folders or Journals

You'll also want to plan a way for students to keep track of their math papers. Here are some ideas:

■ pocket folders—You can buy folders with two interior pockets at very reasonable prices at office-supply stores. Students can keep them in their desks and store both finished and ongoing work. Early in the year, show students where you want them to put names and

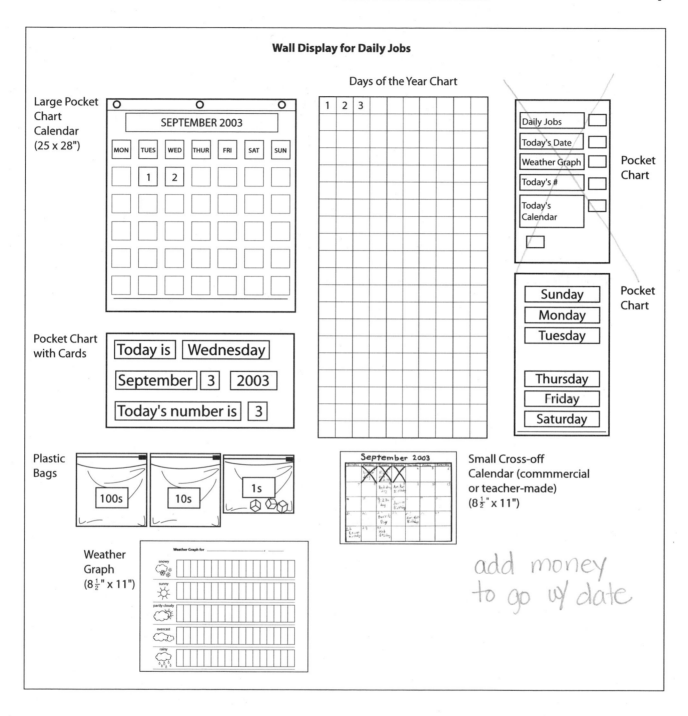

FIGURE 1–3 ▲

dates on each piece of work if you use a loose-leaf system such as this. Pocket folders have the advantage of flexibility, including making it easy for you to collect work from every child on a particular assignment. But you and your students will need to put some effort into keeping the papers organized and to clean out the folders periodically, possibly for a portfolio presentation.

Wall display for daily jobs.

- blank books—You can use commercially available composition books or books you staple together yourself by folding 12-by-18-inch newsprint to form 9-by-12-inch books covered with a piece of construction paper. Students can glue worksheets into these books when appropriate and should date each new piece of work. Blank books have the advantage of keeping work in chronological order and making blank paper readily available to each student. However, they don't have the flexibility inherent in a pocket-folder system and can be unwieldy if you want to check each child's work on a particular assignment.

Students' Developing Number Sense

One way to decide whether you are providing your students with a useful mathematical program is to ask yourself if you are giving them enough opportunities to develop a strong sense of number. This somewhat elusive notion can be defined as the ability to think about numbers efficiently, accurately, flexibly, and with confidence. Having number sense includes:

- being able to take numbers apart and put them back together again—decomposing or partitioning numbers.
- understanding how numbers compare to one another in terms of their relative magnitude.
- having a *conceptual* understanding of the basic mathematical operations of addition, subtraction, multiplication, and division and opportunities to develop algorithms for performing those operations.
- knowing about number relationships.
- being able to make accurate estimates.

It's important to understand how these ideas relate to second grade mathematical concepts.

Composing and Decomposing Numbers

Being able to decompose or partition numbers is what much of primary-number work has focused on. It includes knowing that 7 can be partitioned as 3 + 4, 1 + 6, or 2 + 5. Over time, second graders need to develop confidence that the quantity of the whole has not changed even though they have decomposed the number in many different ways. Once they feel comfortable decomposing smaller numbers, they can apply this thinking toward understanding the structure of larger numbers—knowing, for instance, that 28 can be decomposed into 20 and 8. It is immensely important to give children many opportunities to decompose numbers, both through using concrete models *and* performing the exercise mentally.

Relative Magnitude of Numbers

Second graders should begin to know whether a number is close to or far from a given referent. For example, 24 is almost 25, about half of 50, and small compared to 100. Children develop these understandings by having many opportunities to count quantities of concrete things and to think about the concepts of more and less through games, measuring, number line, and graphing experiences.

Understanding Operations

Second graders need to know that addition involves combining quantities and that subtraction may involve taking something away, or looking at the difference between two quantities. Understanding operations includes knowing when to apply each operation. This ability develops in children when they have many opportunities to solve appropriate word problems. Second graders need frequent occasions to construct their own procedures for applying operations, with chances to develop increasingly efficient methods that make sense to them.

Number Relationships

Understanding number relationships involves grasping the relative magnitude of numbers, as well as operations. For second graders, it includes knowing that if $5 + 5 = 10$, then $5 + 6 = 11$. It also includes such concepts as knowing what happens when you add 10 to any number. Children frequently draw on their understanding of pattern when noticing and analyzing number relationships.

Estimation

Estimating helps children develop number sense because it makes them focus on numbers and how they relate to one another. Estimation also helps children develop that all-important notion of the reasonableness of answers. To develop your second graders' sense of number, ask them often to estimate in terms of a given referent. For example, when posing a question about how many cubes it might take to fill a particular container, you might ask, "Do you think it will take more than a hundred, or fewer than a hundred cubes?"

If children have opportunities to develop these understandings in ways that match their developmental level, they'll become engaged in activities that will help them grow mathematically. The world is filled with experiences that can encourage this growth. In the remaining chapters of this book, you'll find many specific suggestions for activities that develop number sense.

Scheduling Math—Every Day

You'll need to find time in your daily schedule for:

- a morning routine of set activities
- a 45–50-minute block of time sometime later in the day
- unscheduled opportunities throughout the day—whenever you can capitalize on mathematical possibilities that arise within other subject areas

Morning Routines

The morning-routine period lasts for about 20–30 minutes each day. It can work well as an opening activity for the day. It begins with three calendar-related activities (see page 21) and is followed by the activity *Today's Number* (see page 28). Although small variations happen during this time period as the year progresses, these are fairly unchanging routines.

Math Block, Including Menu

Later in the day, but preferably in the morning—when children are most alert—you'll schedule the main math period of the day. This period generally consists of a 15–20-minute discussion period and about a half-hour of time to work on math activities.

The discussion period might consist of introduction of a new activity at the beginning of the session or a follow-up discussion at the end of the period.

The activity period might be a time when all students are working on the same activity, alone or with a partner, or children might be choosing from a menu of activities.

You'll have to see whether these time blocks are a good match for your students. Shorter amounts of time might be better earlier in the year, as students learn to be active listeners and independent problem solvers.

Menu

A menu offers children a choice of two-to-ten activities that you have slowly introduced over time. You can find an example of a menu and ways to introduce it in Chapter 2.

A big advantage of having a menu set-up is that it accommodates children who are working at different rates. Even on a day when you have assigned a particular problem to solve or activity that you want every child to do, youngsters who finish early can be directed to the menu as others finish up. Menus also offer children opportunities to repeat an activity several times, so that they get beyond the procedure of the activity and more deeply into the mathematics. In addition, menus encourage children to take more responsibility for their own learning and to be more self-directed. Finally, once children are working responsibly on a menu, you have more time to observe and assess as you move from table to table during the work period.

Encouragement Throughout the Day

Mathematical exploration should not be confined to scheduled math times. In fact, some of the most exciting mathematical moments that happen in classrooms are often unscheduled and even unexpected. It's all a matter of staying open and alert to possibilities.

For example, brief mathematical side trips can occur during the reading of literature. Second-grade teachers often use the wonderful My Father's Dragon series by Ruth Stiles Gannet as a read-aloud. In addition to recounting adventures suited to the interests of second graders, this series is filled with potential mathematical side trips. For instance, you may want to keep a running record of just how many tangerines Elmer has left after each of his snacks, as he slowly consumes the thirty-one tangerines that he picked before heading over to Wild Island. When Elmer finds himself surprised by "the fourteen green eyes coming out of the jungle" in the book's Chapter 5, you can have children share their thoughts about how many creatures have surrounded the quick-thinking Elmer Elevator.

The big idea? Stay alert to situations in other curricular areas that offer fun, intriguing mathematical inquiry. Also keep your ears open for situations based on your students' interests that could lead to a longer mathematical inquiry. The example below can't be duplicated elsewhere, but I've included it because it illustrates how a student's question can lead to a rich mathematical project in the classroom.

One year, because of a school construction project, my second graders had to walk to and from the playground via a set of stairs commonly known in the community as the ninety-nine steps. Iliana wondered if there really were ninety-nine steps, or if the name was based on the fact that there were a lot of stairs. I asked her how we could find out, and the obvious answer—count the steps—came up. I suggested that at the next recess she make a point of counting them as she ascended them and then check her count on the return trip. She did so, and discovered that she had gotten a different count each time. I gave her two sticky notes and suggested that she record her two counts and show the date that she did them. We found a place on the wall where she could post these two slips of paper under the heading "How Many Steps Did You Count?" We then invited the rest of the class to participate in this data-collection activity by doing their own counting and posting. For the next few weeks, many children counted and posted—none more often than Iliana and her close friend Katy.

One day, as a class, we examined the data. With the children's help, I rearranged the randomly posted notes into a bar graph that let us note the range of counts and the numbers that had come up most often. [The graph looked like the one in Figure 1–4.]

The children easily understood that the counts were inconsistent because the numbers were large and hard to keep track of. Yet we were impressed that the range was fairly small. Because so many pieces of data hovered around ninety-nine, we began to feel fairly certain that an accurate count might very well prove that the steps were aptly named.

Now the problem became how to come up with a definitive count. We finally decided to put one Snap Cube on each step. Iliana and Katy took care of this job and later snapped the cubes into groups of ten. We were thrilled to find out that there were exactly nine groups of ten and nine single cubes left over—ninety-nine steps indeed! Iliana and Katy later wrote up their findings, then posted them in the hallway for other classes to see. What began as a simple question by a curious child had become a full-fledged data-collection-and-analysis exploration that involved many children.

Project Time

Project time is a name for scheduled spontaneity and creativity in the classroom. Three to five times a week, for at least a half-hour to, preferably, forty-five minutes, children get to work on projects of their own choosing. It may help to think of project time as preparation for college, another time in life when students will be asked to devise and develop projects on their own. Your role is to provide materials—crayons; paper; other art materials; and access to building materials such as

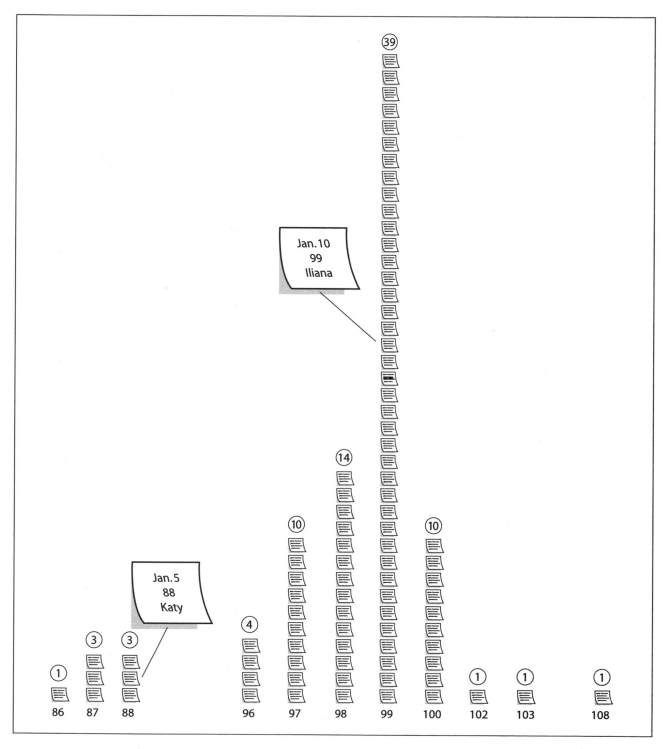

FIGURE 1–4 ▲

Ninety-nine steps data

blocks, Legos, and all the basic math materials you have on hand. You also need to be available to enjoy and respond to your students' creations. Project time is a great way to get to know your students and their interests and to let them know how interested you are in their work. Children love project time. You can help them to understand the importance of being responsible for their own learning through brief discussions at the end of the period. Keep these discussions short and get the kids started by asking volunteers to tell a few things about what they chose to do that day.

Mathematical situations are almost sure to arise once the children have settled into their chosen projects. For example, one day Sonya and Raj were snapping cubes together on the floor, hoping to make a train long enough to go from one side of the room to the other. When they were about halfway across the room, I asked them how many cubes they thought it would take to accomplish the task. They had no firm idea how to estimate the number of cubes needed but were interested in finding the answer. They decided to try counting how many cubes they had used so far. But they found it frustrating to count by ones—they kept getting off track. I asked if there were any other way of counting that might be easier, and they came up with the idea of creating mini-trains of ten cubes each. Their work proceeded over several days, during which they found they could easily store the trains of ten on a tray each day at cleanup time. Eventually, they decided that if they made the last cube of each train blue (they had been using all red cubes), they could tell where each group of ten ended and a new one began. As they worked, many other children became interested in their work. They put aside their pattern-block creations or coloring projects to make estimates of their own about the total cubes needed after learning how many cubes it took to go halfway across the room.

The mathematical richness of the activity developed because Sonya and Raj were working on a project of their own choosing and because they were confronted with an interesting question that they wanted to pursue. So, as teacher, you'll want to stay alert to such possibilities. But also be willing to step back and let the children make final decisions about their own projects.

Thinking About Your Role as Teacher

Perhaps the most important preparation you'll do to get ready for the school year will take place in your own mind. When making choices about your math program, you'll want to remind yourself that your job is to ensure that your students have many opportunities to develop a strong understanding of the world of number. The number of pages you get through in a math workbook won't be the best way to judge your program. Your most important job is to give students a strong conceptual understanding of our number system and a positive attitude about mathematics. One way to judge your program is to continually ask yourself questions such as these: "Am I giving my students many opportunities to compose and decompose numbers? Are my students having experiences that develop their understanding of relative magnitude and number relationships? Have my students had the time to firmly grasp basic mathematical operations?" You'll also want to plan to give some attention to geometry—the mathematical world of shape.

Your students will need to know that you (and their fellow classmates) value their thinking. After providing an appropriate problem to solve, plan to pay close attention to students' reasoning. Be prepared to listen actively and respectfully. When you pay careful attention to your students' ideas, you are more likely to notice and understand how they are thinking. You need this information to know which questions to ask and which problems to pose next. You'll also send the message to your students that you care about and respect their thought process—a powerful message indeed. And you'll model active listening for your students so that they themselves will become better listeners.

Children need to talk about their ideas as they make sense of new concepts. In order for children to feel comfortable talking about their ideas, they need to know that you view mistakes as opportunities to learn and that you value intellectual risk-taking. Remember that your job is not to provide the correct answer, but to guide and question so that children find solutions that lead to the correct answer. Accept that the road to understanding is long and characterized by numerous missteps. Mistakes become learning opportunities when they lead to further exploration. So, when you encounter a mathematical misunderstanding, prepare yourself to say, "Hmm, that's an interesting idea, but I notice . . . ." Then point out how the answer may conflict with some aspect of the problem. Ask "What do you make of that?" to invite the child back into the problem-solving quest.

Perhaps the most difficult and important notion to keep in mind is that students need the luxury of time. They require time to experience a concept in many different ways and to make sense out of the many new concepts they will encounter this year. We all want our students to do well, so we sometimes rush this process. We start feeling need to teach them "the right way" to solve a problem, hoping that this instruction will give them the tool they need to master mathematics. Direct instruction of efficient algorithms seems like such a reasonable thing to do—until you notice how confused students become when asked to do a procedure for which they lack conceptual understanding.

Teaching mathematics in a way that fosters understanding requires a basic trust that children are interested in and capable of understanding mathematical concepts. When you step aside and let students take off in directions that make sense to *them*, you may feel uneasy at first. The reward comes when you see children engaged in mathematical thinking and spontaneously saying, "I really like math!"

Chapter 2

September

GETTING TO KNOW YOU

The first day of school is exciting for students and teachers alike. The second grader is eager to know what school will be like this year—"Will I have friends? Will the work be too hard? What will my teacher be like?" The teacher finally gets to leave behind those end-of-summer nightmares inhabited by unruly children who arrive on a scene where everything is chaos. Instead, she or he arrives early on the first day of school, looking forward to meeting the new class and hopeful that the students will be eager to learn. ∎

The Learning Environment

The next month or so is all about making sure that this year's learning experiences will be positive for everyone. It's about setting ground rules, engaging in easy but significant learning activities, and—most of all—building community. Perhaps your most important job this month is to find ways to let your new students know that you like and respect them—even though in your heart you may be missing the students you had in last year's class! You need to set the stage for a safe environment that promotes friendliness, hard work, and responsibility.

The Mathematics

You'll start September with several days of activities geared toward helping everyone get to know the basic routines and expectations of the classroom. Then you'll present a mathematical menu that will give students a chance to review and use some of their first-grade skills. Throughout the month, the children have a chance to become comfortable in their new classroom and develop both mathematical and social skills.

Classroom Rules: Setting the Stage

Rules provide the structure and reassurance children need and want. As your first order of business on the first day of school, establish class rules. There are many ways to do this important job. Here's one possibility: Introduce simple, straightforward rules, one at a time, giving children plenty of opportunities to discuss the rules and experience following them during that first morning. One of the advantages of this method is that it lets the students know what *you* value and expect. This method also gives *the children* plenty of opportunities to engage with the rules—both through talking about them and doing activities with the rules in mind.

Start with Rule 1, writing it on a piece of paper that will be posted on the wall all year. Your paper might look like this:

In Room 5, it is important to:

1. Be fair and friendly.

Ask for volunteers to contribute ideas about what it means to be fair and friendly, and why these ideas might be important. Solicit several viewpoints to engage the children in a thoughtful discussion. Then explain that this rule is by far the most important, because it has to do with how people treat each other. "If we're fair and friendly to each other, we'll all enjoy school and have many opportunities for learning. Each of us has to do our part in keeping this rule, so we all feel safe and happy."

Next, add Rule 2 to the list:

In Room 5, it is important to:

1. Be fair and friendly.

2. **Work thoughtfully.**

Again, ask for volunteers to explain what this rule means in their own words, and tell why they think it's important. When it's your turn, explain that it's OK to make mistakes and that a mistake can often help us learn. But point out that each person will be expected to put thought and effort into class assignments and projects. "When you work thoughtfully, you give yourself a chance to do your very best work. And you have more opportunities for learning." As with Rule 1, try to help the children see how this rule benefits each of them. Introduce the phrase *business-talk only*, explaining that part of working thoughtfully is staying focused on the job at hand and not having extraneous conversations.

Now it's time to put some of these ideas into practice. Introduce a simple activity, such as drawing a self-portrait (discussed more fully on page 36) as a way to practice being friendly and fair and working thoughtfully. Tying rules an activities gives vitality to the ideas underlying each rule, making them feel real and useful to the children. Sometime during the course of the activity, say something like, "Are you remembering to work thoughtfully?" or "How are you remembering to be fair and friendly?" If students start to chat about something other than the assigned task, say, "Remember, this is a business-talk only time."

When the activity is complete, spend a few minutes discussing the ways people used these rules or noticed others using them. If problems came up during the activity, discuss these, too. But keep the focus on how we can learn from the problems.

Save Rule 3 for the first time that you work with the math manipulatives in the classroom, probably right before you give the children a chance to explore the materials. Your rule list might now look like this:

In Room 5, it is important to:

1. Be fair and friendly.

2. Work thoughtfully.

3. **Take care of materials.**

Again, discuss what this rule looks like in action and why it's important. Spend time looking at where materials are stored, where they can be used, and how they should be handled. Your goal is to set the stage for using the materials thoughtfully and preparing students to take responsibility for getting materials out and putting them away responsibly. Make sure you have in mind how many people can comfortably work with a given material. This number will depend at least partly on how much of each material you have on hand and in the space available in your classroom.

Once you've introduced these first three ground rules, let the children begin exploring the materials. While they're working, note whether you made good planning decisions about how classroom space is used. After this session, take time to discuss the activity in the light of the rule about taking care of materials. If you see that you need to make some changes for the future, take this opportunity to talk about learning from mistakes. You might say something like, "I don't think it was a good idea to suggest that you work on the floor near the bookcase. That made it hard for others to get things off the shelf. I've learned from my mistake and next time I'd like you to . . . ."

Introduce the final rule right before project time—a period of the day when children choose their own projects to work on. Your list might now look like this:

In Room 5, it is important to:

1. Be fair and friendly.

2. Work thoughtfully.

3. Take care of materials.

4. Start work and clean up in a timely way.

Take some time to talk about what it means to work and clean up in a timely way. Make it clear that the rule involves everything from getting one's name on one's paper right away when written work is assigned, to dismantling one's pattern-block designs when project time is over.

You'll probably have to review this rule many times, especially the cleaning-up portion. Children who are deeply engaged in an activity may find it difficult to stop what they're doing and move on to something new just because the clock says it's time. You may also need to have individual conferences with children who consistently bend the clean-up portion of the rule. The most effective consequence of failing to abide by this rule may be to spend time talking about the rule, with you, while the other children busily engage in project time. Try to make these conferences serious discussions of the importance of the rule, rather than finger-wagging sessions.

You may want to work out a five-minute warning system, such as turning off one light or ringing a bell, so that the children feel more in control of the final minutes of their work time. Hold everyone to this rule, reminding the kids that although work must stop now, project time will come again. Also, provide a place for students to store ongoing projects so that work doesn't always have to start from the beginning each day. This probably won't be possible with pattern-block structures, for instance, so children do need to come to grips with the expectation that Rule 4 benefits the entire class.

You may prefer to draw the rules out of the children themselves—another perfectly valid way to set the stage for responsible learning. But whatever method you use, remember that classroom discussions about the rules need to occur frequently during the first few months of school. Use these discussions to notice ways in which the rules are helping students be happy and productive. Discussions also provide opportunities to review the reasons behind the rules and to address any rough spots that have come up.

Daily Jobs

Four daily jobs, centered on two calendars and one (initially) blank number chart, help children develop awareness of patterns both in the yearly cycle and in our number system. Four children each day have an opportunity to come to the front of the class, each to take care of one job. The wall display required to track these activities is described and shown in the "Setting Up the Mathematics Classroom" section in Chapter 1. Each day four new children participate. Rotate their names through the jobs chart in alphabetical order.

Job 1: Today's Date

The first child stands in front of the class, checks to make sure that her classmates are focused on her, and then points to the words in the pocket chart that say:

Today's Date is Wednesday
September 3, 2003

The class reads the words along with her. She then crosses out today's date on the small commercial (or hand-made) calendar posted nearby. (See Blackline Masters.)

Job 2: Weather Graph

Meanwhile, the second child assumes a seat at the front of the class, ready to ask a question such as "What do you think the weather will be like today?" After calling on three classmates for their predictions, he goes to a designated spot to check the sky and makes a decision about what to mark on the class weather graph. (You'll need to choose that designated spot beforehand, based on the child's ability to scan the sky and your sense that it's a safe place for him to be for a few moments. In my California classroom, this is outdoors, at the end of our short hallway. But you may prefer to have your students use a classroom window.) He then returns to the seat at the front of the room, and waits quietly until there's a good time to tell his decision and mark it on the weather graph—usually after the *Days-of-the-Year Number* activity (described below) has been completed.

Job 3: Days-of-the-Year Number

A third child now gets the class's attention and leads students in reading:

Today's number is 1 .

She then adds a counter to the "1s" receptacle. (As time goes on and more counters are added, she must also check to see if there are now enough "1s" to bundle or snap together to make a new group of ten.) During this job routine, based on the number of 1s (and eventually 10s and 100s) reported by the student, fill in the box on the (initially blank) Days-of-the-Year Chart—the one that has ten spaces across each row and enough rows so that there is a box for each day of the school year.

It helps to have language to talk about how the counters and the written expression of quantities relate to one another. One of my students suggested that the written number is a way of "spelling" the number of counters in the receptacles. This terminology seemed to help the children see the connection between the counters and the written number. So now my students and I talk about making sure that we have the right number of counters and that I have "spelled" the number correctly. When the day is over, use these cards to form a horizontal number line, perhaps taping them high around the perimeter of your room.

Job 4: Calendar

The fourth child's job doesn't happen until the end of the day, when he is asked to announce something significant about the day. His statement will be recorded on the month-long pocket calendar. Early in the day, announce who will be making the day's statement. That way, the designated child can begin thinking about what he would like to say. Sometime in the afternoon, ask him to reflect on the day and dictate a statement. Early in the year, you might want to let the child in charge of this job ask for suggestions from the class at large. Later in the year, you can probably expect greater independence. You (or the child) will write the statement on a square of paper that corresponds to today's date and is just large enough to place over the day's date in the pocket calendar posted in front of the room. The child draws a picture to illustrate the statement, then places the square in its appropriate spot on the calendar. (See Figure 2–1.)

At the close of each day, after the children have been dismissed, take a moment to get the wall display set up for the next day. Change the date, *Today's Number*, and the student names in the daily jobs chart. Move the old *Today's Number* card to the spot in your room where you've decided to begin your growing number line.

At the end of the month, remove the squares from the pocket calendar in order and then bind them together to make a new minibook for the class library. (If you don't have access to a binder, a hole can be punched in the corner of each page and a thick piece of yarn used to hold the pages together.)

At the beginning of the year, you'll need to model how to do each job. Address such issues as where a person needs to stand (in order to leave a clear view for others) while leading the class in reading a sentence. You may even want to discuss such issues as the path that would be "most polite" for a student to take as she comes up to the board. Encourage

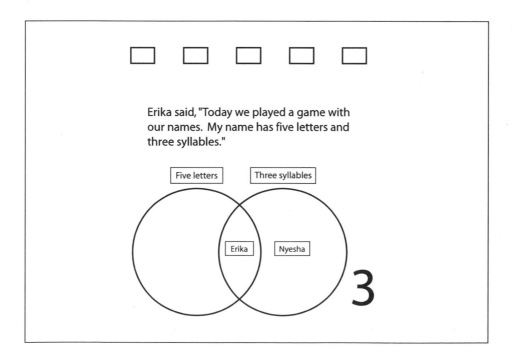

FIGURE 2–1 ◄

A sample calendar page.

students to be aware of when they're accidentally interrupting the group; you'll send a clear message about being considerate of others. But as the year progresses, try to remove yourself as much as possible from these routines. As you get to know your students, you'll find out who needs a little assistance getting the classes' attention and performing the jobs. Still, emphasize the notion that your students can assume more and more responsibility by staying on the sidelines as much as possible.

Once the three morning jobs have been performed, take a few minutes to develop mathematical ideas by suggesting one of or more of these activities on any given day:

- Look for patterns on the number chart.
- Chant the days of the week.
- Discuss the difference between the calendar date and the days-of-the-year number. Why aren't they the same? Or, if they *are* the same number, will they always be the same?)
- At the beginning of one month, remove all the numbers from the one-month pocket calendar and have the students build the calendar with you. The idea is to put the numbers in the appropriate boxes. But once the position of the 1 is established, you can ask a child to figure out where the 5 belongs, then where the 8 belongs, and so on—until all the numbers are placed (Sheffield 2001).
- Connect the number of counters (in the 1s, 10s, and 100s places) with the number in the pocket chart and with digits you're writing in the number chart. Children find it easy to fall into a routine of "reading" the charts without attending to numbers' meaning. Make the point that the symbolic representation of the number is a way of "spelling" the number and reflects the number of counters in the cups. For example, you might say, "So you counted eight ones after you added a counter for today. I'll write an eight here. Now did you say there were two tens? I'll write that here next to the eight. Now we've got two tens and eight ones. The fast way to say that is (pause) twenty-eight."

Name Sorting: A Community-Building Activity

Second graders are highly invested in their names. You can use their interest to:

- provide a community-building activity that enables students to get to know one another's names—and one another.

- explore sorting concepts that are essential to logical/mathematical growth.
- combine math and reading concepts in one activity.

Materials

- 8-inch lengths of sentence strip, 1 for each student and 1 for yourself
- 3 or 4 large sticky notes for each student
- loops of yarn, each 3 yards long, in 3 different colors

Instructions: Day 1

1. Write your first name on one of the pieces of sentence strip and display it as a model. Emphasize that you started your name with an uppercase letter and used lowercase for all the other letters.

2. Explain that the students are going to be playing sorting games using their first names. Have each child write her or his first name neatly on the sentence strip. For best results, it helps to have teacher-prepared name tags with both first and last names at each child's seat. Have the children write their names first in pencil, using your model to copy from, and then trace over their work with crayon or marker.

3. Explain that you've noticed several interesting things about your own name. If your name is Nancy, for instance, you might say (and record on the board) things like:

   "My name begins with an *N*."

   "My name has two syllables (Clap out the syllables of your name and several other names in the classroom to ensure your students understand what a syllable is.)

   "My name has five letters."

   "My name has two vowels."

   "My name has a *short a* in it."

   "The other vowel in my name is *y*, but it makes the sound of *e* at the end of my name."

   As you're talking about your name, the children will likely start discussing their own names. If they come up with additional ideas, such as *long a* or *silent e*, list these ideas on a separate part of the board.

4. Ask the children to think of at least three interesting things about their names and record each idea on a separate sticky note. They should use the words you've written on the board as models, but not confine themselves to the ideas on the board.

5. End this part of the lesson by collecting all the sticky notes. Have the children place their name tags in the middle of their tables for easy access in the future.

Instructions: Day 2

1. Sort through all the sticky notes, recording each new idea on a piece of heavy tag. These will become labels for the next part of the lesson.

2. Pick out two labels, such as *has three syllables* and *has three letters*. Look for two ideas that are mutually exclusive, so that no child's name will fit under both labels.

3. Have the children sit in a circle on the rug, bringing their names tags with them. You might want to give the children an opportunity to talk about their names among themselves for a moment. Meanwhile, form two side-by-side yarn circles in the center of the rug, where everyone can see them. Call the group to attention and then choose a label for each circle. Explain your choices. For example, say, "The red circle is for names that have three *letters*. The yellow circle is for names that have three *syllables*." Ask each child in turn to decide if her or his name belongs in either circle. If it does, have the student put the name tag in the appropriate circle. (See Figure 2–2.)

4. When all the names have been placed, say, "We call this way of organizing data a Venn diagram. It's called a Venn diagram because a person whose last name was Venn came up with this kind of graphic representation. Where do you think your name belongs on the Venn diagram if it doesn't go in either circle?" If no one responds, explain that names that don't belong inside either circle can go outside the circles.

FIGURE 2–2   ▶

A Venn diagram without an intersection.

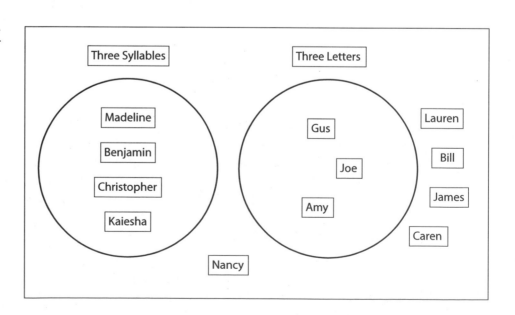

5. Now spend a few moments talking about what this arrangement allows you to observe. Such ideas might come up:

   ■ Only three people have three letters in their names.

   ■ There are more people who have three syllables than have three letters.

   ■ Most people don't belong in either circle.

6. Have each child retrieve his or her name tag while you choose two new labels for the two circles. You might choose two mutually exclusive categories. Or, if you feel that your students are ready to think about the concept of an intersection, choose two inclusive categories. For example, categories such as *has five letters* and *has two syllables* are likely to yield names that fit in both circles.

7. Once again, introduce the two categories. When some children realize the dilemma of needing to put their names in both circles, they will likely place their names straddling both circles. Ask, "What could we do to fit Clara's name in both circles at the same time?" Let your students struggle with this problem and offer whatever suggestions they may have. If no one comes up with the idea of overlapping the two circles, suggest it yourself and introduce the term *intersection*. (See Figure 2–3.)

8. When everyone's name is placed appropriately, discuss what this arrangement reveals about the names in your class. Continue resorting names for as long as there is interest in the activity. Repeat this

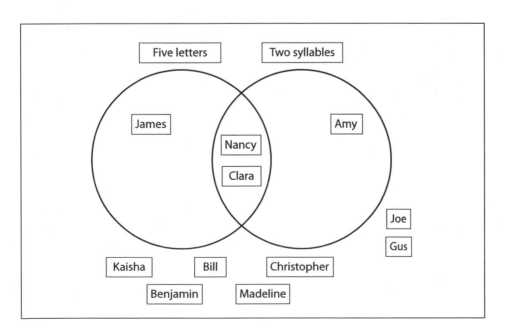

FIGURE 2-3 ◀

A Venn diagram with an intersection.

activity several times in the next few weeks, possibly adding new categories as you explore new phonetic ideas with your class.

Today's Number: A Daily Routine

Number sense is vital to any math student. One way to help your students develop number sense is to have them write daily equations relating to a designated number. You can use either the calendar date as your target number or write equations that correspond to the number of days you've been in school.

Getting Started

Prepare a composition book for each child, consisting of pages with a simple cover that looks something like this:

Today's Number

   A Book of Equations
   by
   _____

On about the fifth day of school (or early in the month), write the numeral *5* and the word *five* on the chalkboard (or on a piece of chart paper if you want to save the equations each day). Ask if anyone has another way to make 5. You'll likely get a volunteer who suggests $3 + 2 = 5$ or a similar two-addend equation. Add this equation to the board and continue gathering ideas until you have three or four equations on the board.

Now ask the children to write their names on the front of their composition book, open the book to the first page, and write the same heading that you've written on the board (*5 five*). Give them a few minutes to write some of their own equations for 5, or to copy some of the equations from the board. Suggest that they might want to get cubes or other manipulatives to come up with new ideas. While the children are working, circulate among the tables. Make simple comments, such as "What's your first equation going to be?" to help reluctant starters begin.

Bring the group back together and spend a few moments recording additional equations on the board. As you do this, express enthusiasm about the students' thinking, without praising one's child's effort more than another's. Comments that focus on the mathematics are most helpful, especially when you record children's efforts on the board at the same time, and can include things like this:

"Four plus one equals five. That's an important idea in mathematics—
it's what counting by ones is all about. When we count on from one
number to the next, we're always adding one more."

"Three plus two equals five, and two plus three equals five. This is a
big idea in addition—you can put the same numbers in a different
order, and they still add up to the same amount. Can anyone think of
another example that shows this idea?"

End the lesson by telling the children where to put their equation books
and when you'll be doing the activity each day.

Establishing the *Today's Number* Routine

Today's Number is an activity that can take place at the same time every
day, possibly as a warm-up when the children arrive at school or when
they return to the classroom from recess or some other outside activity.

The daily routine looks like this:

1. Announce the number for the day.

2. Pose the question, "Who has an idea for an equation for today's
   number?" Elicit a few responses to get the thinking started. Then
   have the children begin their independent work at their seats.

3. The children write the day's number as a heading on the next page
   of their composition books and write individual equations for that
   number in their books, using cubes or other manipulatives if they so
   choose.

4. Students bring their books to a circle on the rug and discuss equations as you record them on the chalkboard or on a piece of chart
   paper. You ask the children to explain their thinking about their
   own equations or those of other students that have been recorded
   on the board. You also take the opportunity to expand on ideas that
   the children are exploring.

Supporting Students

Your presence will be important as the children work in their equation
books. Students will overhear your conversations with individual children
as you circulate among the tables commenting on the work. Saying something like, "I notice you're using a pattern to make subtraction equations.
You started with ten minus zero equals ten, and then did eleven minus one
equals ten and then twelve minus two equals ten. What will your next
equation be?" will support the learning of the child you're speaking to
and may also pique the interest of other children nearby.

Children will likely come to you and ask, "Does this equation work?" After checking the equation, you may respond, "Yes, it does. Can you convince yourself that it does?" At that point, you may get an unexpected response. For instance, a child may offer this explanation for the equation $6 + 8 - 7 = 7$: "Well, when I took the seven away, I left one behind from the eight and I know that six plus one equals seven." This shows a growing understanding of number relationships—a major achievement. The answer is unexpected, because another person might look at the same equation and say, "Six plus eight equals fourteen, and fourteen minus seven equals seven. So, yes, the equation is correct." Talking with the children will give you insight into how they are thinking and will open your eyes to the many varied ways children think about number.

Or, you might discover that an equation is incorrect. So your response could be, "I see a problem with that equation. See if you can figure out what I mean. This can be an opportunity for you to learn. Let me know what you find out." This kind of encounter can reinforce the notion that mistakes aren't bad—rather, they're valuable opportunities to learn.

Confusion is a natural part of the learning process, and in general you don't want to be too directive in your teaching. But that doesn't mean you should leave children floundering helplessly. Stay alert for children who get stuck. Offer them suggestions, such as, "Try getting out six cubes to get started. Now, try putting those six cubes into two groups. How many do you have in this group? It's OK to touch the cubes as you count them. Umm, so four here. How many in the other group? So two there. Now you can write the equation four plus two equals six." Check back with these students frequently until they develop strategies that make them more independent. Confidence in their ability to do the task is tremendously important to these children. It can help them develop the persistence they'll need to make progress in a challenging curriculum.

Being available to children during this activity will also help them deal with some of the emotions that may come up. A child who feels upset that someone else has "stolen my equation" can receive recognition for coming up with an interesting idea—but remind her that no one owns a mathematical idea. Say, "We're all in this together. The idea is to learn from one another. If someone has the same equation as you, it might mean that they had the same idea, or that you've helped him or her learn something new. Giving each other good ideas is one of the reasons we do this activity."

Recording Equations on the Board

By taking about ten minutes a day to have students share their equations in a group setting, you accomplish several things:

- You give students many opportunities to verbalize their thinking so they learn to describe their problem-solving strategies.

- You give them opportunities to learn from one another. It's not always possible for one person to follow another's line of thought. Yet ideas presented by one child often prompt other children to develop new ways of thinking.

- You give yourself opportunities to expand on an idea presented by a child, and thereby help students make important mathematical connections.

But before children share their equations for you to record on the chalkboard, discuss the notion of *respectfully* disagreeing with a classmate. Ask, "Who has an idea for what you might say if you disagree with a classmate's equation? How can you share your mathematical idea without putting down your classmate? Think about the tone of voice you might use, as well as the words you might say." Let a few volunteers give their ideas, supporting those ideas that use matter-of-fact language and a friendly tone of voice. Conclude the discussion by saying something like, "If you offer your ideas in a friendly way, you give your classmate a chance to learn and that's the whole purpose of this activity."

While recording equations on the chalkboard, stop frequently and ask questions such as, "Can you prove that your equation is true?" or "Do you agree that this equation is true? What makes you think that? Did someone else think about it in a different way?"

For example, one child might offer this equation:

$$5 + 5 + 5 + 5 + 1 = 21$$

You ask: "How did you convince yourself that this equation works?" The child answers: "Well, I went five, ten, fifteen, twenty, and one more is twenty-one." While the child is talking, you write these numbers under the appropriate parts of the equation. Then you say: "Does anyone have another way of explaining this equation?" A volunteer might say: "I see five plus five equals ten, and then there's another five plus five equals ten. Now you have twenty, because ten plus ten equals twenty. Then one more is twenty-one." As the child speaks, record these equations or draw lines below the appropriate parts of the original equation showing how the child has combined the 5s to make 10s:

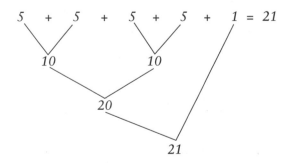

Then ask: "Can this equation help us make other equations that work?" This query could lead to:

10 + 10 + 1 = 21

5 + 5 + 5 + 6 = 21

8 + 2 + 8 + 2 + 1 = 21

This last equation could lead to 8 + 2 + 10 + 1 = 21, which could lead to 8 + 2 + 11 = 21.

If no one offers ideas, you can put one of these equations on the board and ask if anyone sees a connection with the original equation.

Wait time becomes crucial at this point. Make sure that many children, not just the quickest, have time to reflect on these ideas. You may need to remind students to keep their thinking inside their heads until others have had enough time to make a decision. When several hands have gone up, ask for a volunteer to respond.

Throughout the lesson, look for opportunities to help students see new ways to decompose numbers, notice number relationships, and use mathematical operations meaningfully.

If a child offers an incorrect equation, he or she will often discover the mistake while talking about it. If a student becomes confused or flustered, offer an opportunity to think about it alone. Say, "We'll get back to you when you're ready. This is one of those opportunities to learn from a mistake."

Expanding Students' Thinking About Equations

The *Today's Number* activity is similar to the routines in the TERC series Investigations in Number, Data, and Space. The developers of this second-grade curriculum suggest that students follow certain guidelines to get extra practice on concepts you introduce in your current curriculum. So, for example, you might say:

"Use only addition."

"Use only subtraction."

"Use both addition and subtraction."

"Use combinations of ten [7 + 3 + 8 + 2 + 1 = 21]."

"Use doubles [4 + 4 + 3 + 3 + 5 + 5 + 2 = 26]."

"Use multiples of five [5 + 10 + 25 = 40]."

"Use only two addends [125 + 15 = 140 or 139 + 1 = 140]." (Introduce this guideline later in the year, when you're working on double-digit addition.)

Your students may moan and groan at these restrictions, but they'll also be pushed to new understandings. Still, make sure that you have plenty of days on which there are no rules.

Including Everyone

Once you establish the *Today's Number* routine and more and more children begin offering equations, explain that you're going to start checking off the names of everyone who has had a turn. Explain that you want to be fair and include every student. You may discover that some children never offer equations and therefore have no checks by their names. Reiterate that you want to make sure everyone is included. Let those students who have not participated know that sometime soon you'd like an equation from them. Check with them the next day, as they're formulating equations in their books, and invite them to talk about an equation they're exploring.

Keeping Yourself Sane

By recording equations in their own books, children feel in charge of the mechanics of this activity. But this strategy does have a pitfall. Over the course of the year, children are going to make mistakes as they think through new ideas. These mistakes get recorded in their books. You'll catch many of these errors as you circulate among the children each day. But remind yourself that such mistakes are OK and that *you don't have time to correct each child's book every day.*

Remind yourself, also, that this routine is a playful way for the children to *develop* number understandings. It's not a testing situation in which mistakes are counted. What's written in the book is not nearly as important as what the children learn by trying out new ideas and listening to one another during class discussion about the equations. If you feel uncomfortable with uncorrected errors, have the kids jot their ideas down on scratch paper and toss the paper in the recycling bin at the end of each day. It's what happens between their ears—not what they record on paper—that matters.

Monthly Calendars

Early every month, you may want to give your students a chance to make their own take-home calendar. This calendar might consist of a seasonal drawing on 8-by-11-inch paper and a calendar grid. (Use the Blackline Master for the hand-made calendar that the class crosses off each day.) The child fills in the grid with the days of the month, special school events, and classmates' birthdays. The finished product can be mounted on a piece of 12-by-18-inch construction paper. Prepare for this activity by making a model calendar yourself and writing key information on the board such as:

September 2003

> September begins on a Monday.
>
> September has 30 days.
>
> 2—First day of School
>
> 14—Knesha's birthday
>
> 18—Back-to-School Night
>
> 19—Evan's birthday

Go over the information you've listed, discussing why you indicated that September begins on a Monday and has thirty days. Show your model of the calendar, pointing out how you fit in the special events in the appropriate date boxes. Suggest that students fill in the calendar grid first, and then add a drawing made on a plain piece of paper. Brainstorm possible topics for the drawing, such as a late summer tree, your school building, etc. When both parts of the calendar are complete, students can glue them to a large sheet of construction paper. At home, they can add information for the month that pertains to their families; for example, siblings' or parents' birthdays.

This task encourages students to be organized and follow directions. Note who is able to complete the task with ease and who has problems placing the numbers in order and in the right place. You'll gain important information about your students' organizational abilities. (See Figure 2–4.)

Time Capsules

Creating individual "time capsules" filled with selected objects and school projects can help children grasp the notion that, over time, the class will be creating a history together. This activity promotes a sense of community early in the year as students help one another measure their heights, find positive ways to discuss each other's work, choose items to set aside, and look to the future. When you look at these items later in the year, you

FIGURE 2-4 ◄

A child's calendar

can gauge individual progress. By comparing their September and June work, children themselves become thoughtful, reflective learners who strive to do their best and enjoy observing their own growth.

To create a time capsule, you'll need gallon-sized plastic bags or file folders, labeled with each child's name, in which they will store their items for the year. Explain the concept of a time capsule, and let the children know that each of them will be opening his or her own capsule at the end of the school year.

What goes into the time capsules? Below are a few suggestions, though you and your students might want to come up with additional ideas. Choose items that take into account your students' current skill level. Make sure your choices create an opportunity to build confidence and set the tone for working thoughtfully.

Self-Portraits

This item was mentioned in the "Classroom Rules" section earlier in this chapter. In addition to talking to the children about working thoughtfully on their self-portraits, you might *briefly* discuss some artistic elements of the task. Have mirrors available so that children can notice the shape of their faces—round, oval, etc. Suggest that they start by drawing a shape that is similar to the shape of their own faces. Have the children feel where their eyes are and notice where other facial features are in relationship to the eyes. Talk about how ears are at about the same level as eyes, and note details such as eyebrows and eyelashes. Let each child decide whether to do a full body portrait or head only. Emphasize that a portrait is not a photograph and therefore will not be an exact likeness. Before the children share their work with the class by posting it on a bulletin board, talk about appropriate comments that they might make about each other's portraits. Model such language as, "I notice that Ailey used several different colors to make her hair color look realistic," and "The shape of Eric's face in his portrait is a good match for his real face." Talk about how comments such as, "Margie's is the best!" may make another student feel that his or her work is inferior.

Body Measurements

Have children work in pairs to measure each other. Demonstrate this task by lying down on the floor (or asking a child to do this) and then having a child cut a string that matches your height. Children can simply save their strings in a plastic bag. To quantify their height, children can determine how many interlocking cubes it takes to make a train the same length of the string.

Handprints

Kids can crate handprints by tracing around their hand or by making a plaster impression. They might also use tempera paint to make a print. They can quantify the size of the handprint by seeing how many beans, tiles, or cubes it takes to cover the image.

Writing Samples

Choose a topic for everyone to write about, or just encourage each child to save his or her first writing effort of the year. Topics might include *My Hopes for Second Grade* or other ideas students want to use. Remind reluctant youngsters that they're going to have a whole year to grow as writers. Tell them that this first sample just needs to be their best effort for now.

Number-Games Menu: Activities for the Rest of the Month

Number games encourage children to become proficient with single-digit addition and subtraction through repeated *use*, not drill, and provide an engaging context for learning. Games also serve as a reminder that children should use mathematics, not simply endure it. And by teaching children to choose from a menu of activities, you encourage them to take responsibility for their own learning and work cooperatively. They learn how to make decisions and how to take care of materials. After learning the ropes, your students will be able to do this menu on their own—and will be prepared to take on more complex, independent activities later in the year.

Setting the Stage

Before playing any games involving competition, discuss how it feels to be a "winner" and a "loser." Have your students suggest appropriate behavior for both roles. Make sure that you or one of the children contributes these kinds of suggestions to the conversation:

- "Losers" can remind themselves that these are just games and that accepting losses quickly means they have more time to play again— and possibly be winners.

- "Winners" need to think through the importance of not gloating. Say something like, "When you win, you'll probably feel great. You can say to yourself, 'Wow, I really enjoyed winning that game.' But don't make a big deal of it out loud. Being fair and friendly means finding a way to feel good without making your partner feel put down."
- Playing games is fun, but the focus needs to be on the mathematics. The real reason for playing number games is to become better mathematicians.

You may also want to discuss early on how to decide quickly and fairly who gets to go first when playing a game (or how to decide which game to play). When you bring these issues up, you'll probably get suggestions such as: "It's polite to let your partner choose." "You can do *Rock, Paper, Scissors.*" "You can ask someone else to pick a number ten or less and see who gets the closest." Don't let the class get too hung up on this matter; remind the children that the key is to begin playing the game to get the most fun and learning out of it. Having this kind of discussion before any problems occur will help students avoid unproductive behavior later.

Menu Schedule

Your plan for introducing a number-games menu might look something like this:

- Day 1: Model how to play one of the games with a student, and then have everyone play that game with a partner.
- Day 2: Model a second game, and have everyone play the new game.
- Day 3: Have students choose Game 1 or Game 2. A few minutes before the end of the session, have students clean up and have a follow-up discussion.
- Day 4: Teach a third game, and have everyone play it.
- Day 5: Have students choose among the three games. At the end of the period, discuss one or more of the games.
- Subsequent days: Continue to add games as interest in the previously introduced games wanes. As you plan your day, keep in mind that the 45-minute math period should include about 30 minutes to play games and about 15 minutes for either introducing a new game or discussing strategies from a previous game.

You may want to spend two or three solid weeks on this menu during September. Or, spend less time on it now and then come back to it periodically throughout the year as you teach new games. Spend enough time so that students become comfortable with making choices, working with a partner, and taking care of materials before you move on to other things. And don't forget to have the menu materials readily available for those times when you are absent and want the kids to continue the games with a substitute teacher.

Introducing New Games

When you introduce a game, you set the stage for students to work thoughtfully and get the most learning out of the experience. Here's an example of how you might demonstrate playing the *Adding and Subtracting* game. By the way, this game was devised by two second-grade boys. They developed it as part of a probability unit, described in Chapter 4 of this book. The rules below are as they wrote them, with only their spelling edited; an edited version follows.

The Adding and Subtracting Game
by Aaron and Colby

You need: Two dice and a piece of paper

Instructions:

If you roll, for example, 6 and 5, you get one point from the difference between 6 and 5. And you get 11 because 6 + 5 = 11. So your score would be 12.

Or, for another example, if you get 3 and 2, you would get one point from the difference between 3 and 2. And you would get 5 because 3 + 2 = 5. So your score would be 6.

You each roll 8 times by taking turns.

And player 1 rolls first.

And if you get a double such as 1 + 1, you only get 2 because there is no difference between 1 and 1.

The game is over when each player rolls 8 times.

Use the calculator to add up the final score for each player.

Adding and Subtracting

Materials

- 2 dice
- 1 piece of paper

Instructions

1. Gather students in a circle on the rug.

2. Ask for a volunteer (or invite a child) to demonstrate the game by playing it with you. For the demonstration round, explain that in this game you score points by rolling two dice. You get points by first

adding the two dice together to find the sum of the two. You also need to find the difference between the two. Determine your *total score* for each round by adding together the sum *and* the difference.

3. Have one person roll the dice and tell the class what numbers came up. Let's assume that she rolled a six and a five. Say, "Raise your hand if you would like to explain how to add six and five." Pick a volunteer to tell both the answer and the way he arrived at the answer. Ask at least one other person to share her answer and strategy for getting the answer. You're likely to get ideas such as, "I know that five plus five is ten, so I just added one more because six is one more than five" and "I started with the six and counted up five more to get eleven."

   By expressing these ideas verbally, children become comfortable sharing their strategies with one another. If you don't get these suggestions, say them yourself to model what you mean when you ask someone to tell how he or she got an answer.

4. Continue the demonstration by saying, "Now we have to figure out the difference between the two numbers. Does anyone have an idea?" Make sure you call on girls as frequently as boys, and remind yourself to call on girls first as often as you call on boys. After you've had some volunteers explain how they got the answer, use the chalkboard or overhead to show how the children will record their scores once the game begins. Your example might look like this:

Julie	*Pietr*
Round one: $6 + 5 = 11$	$4 + 3 = 7$
$6 - 5 = 1$	$4 - 3 = 1$
Total score: $11 + 1 = 12$	$7 + 1 = 8$

5. Explain that a round is finished when both partners have rolled the dice and determined their scores. Do another demonstration or two, discussing strategies for figuring out the score and modeling what needs to be recorded. Announce that a complete game requires eight rounds, then ask if anyone has questions about how to play.

6. Next, go over your expectations for setting up the recording sheets. Then let the fun begin—with a gentle reminder that everyone is expected to work thoughtfully.

Conducting Follow-Up Discussions

After the class has played *Adding and Subtracting*—or any other game— three or four times, spend some time talking about the game's mathematics. For example, with *Adding and Subtracting*, you might ask,

"Which combination of numbers gave you your best score?"

"Which combinations gave you your smallest score?"

"Did you ever get the same score, but with different combinations of numbers?" (If you look at all the possible combinations, you'll find that anytime you roll a six, no matter what the other number is, you'll get a score of 12. Ask, "Is that true of other numbers?")

"Do you see any patterns as you look at combinations and the scores they give you?" There are interesting patterns to see here. For example, if you roll a 5 on one die, with one exception, you'll always get a score of 10. Here's the pattern:

die 1	die 2	addition	subtraction	total score
5	1	6	4	10
5	2	7	3	10
5	3	8	2	10
5	4	1	9	10
5	5	0	10	10
5	6	1	11	12

Decide how to explore them with students based on their interest and current mathematical understandings.

Questions to Discuss

Here are some questions you can use to spark discussion about any game:

"How are you and your partner working out differences?"

"How is your partner (or you) making this activity fun and productive for you as learners?"

"Is this a game of chance or skill, or both?"

"What strategies are you using to win the game?"

"After you played the game several times, did your strategies change? If so, why?"

"How did you add (or subtract) the numbers?"

"What are you learning from this game?"

Additional Number Games

Here are some other possible games to add to your menu. As always, feel free to add others that you like to teach. (See the Blackline Masters for reproducible versions.)

Sweet Thirteen

Materials

- 1 deck of cards, with face cards removed

Instructions

1. Shuffle the cards, then deal seven cards to each player.

2. Leave the rest of the cards face down. This is the draw pile.

3 Player 1: Choose one of the cards in your hand, and place it face up next to the draw pile. Say the value of the card out loud.

4. Player 2: Place one of your cards next to the first one, and add its value to the first card. If the total value is more than thirteen, draw from the pile until you get a card you can play that brings the total to thirteen or less. Say the total value out loud when you're done.

5. Play continues until one player brings the total of the two face-up cards to exactly thirteen. That player sets the trick aside and gets to lead with a new card.

6. The player to get rid of all his or her cards first is the winner.

Note: This game can go on for a long time, as students have to go to the draw pile for a card with a small enough value to play. By holding onto small-value cards, a player can avoid having to go to the draw pile so often. This strategy may become quickly obvious to adults, but it eludes many second graders. Rather than "teach" this strategy, have some classroom discussions in which you ask students to tell which cards they want to hold onto. Don't be surprised if some children truly feel that keeping larger numbers is a good idea—the notion that bigger is best is compelling to a second grader!

Odd or Even?

Materials

- 1 deck of cards, with face cards removed

Instructions

Two partners will be working together, against the deck. Players might want to keep track of how many times they win and how many times the deck wins. The object of the game is to remove all the cards from play by going through the deck only one time.

1. Shuffle the cards, then take the top two cards and place them face up, side by side and slightly overlapping one another. Set the rest of the deck face down next to the two cards.

2. If the sum of the two face-up cards is an *even number*, remove them from play and turn over two more cards from the deck. If the sum is an *odd number*, take a third card from the deck and place it face up, slightly overlapping the top card.

3. If the sum of the top two cards is *now* even, remove them from play. If the sum is odd, add another card—once again slightly overlapping the three cards already face up.

4. Continue in this fashion, always looking only at the top two cards, until you have used up all the cards in the deck.

5. Make a note of who won—you or the deck!

Note: This game offers lots of practice in addition. It's also an opportunity to explore properties of odd and even numbers. For example, do you get an odd or an even number when you add two even numbers? What happens when you add two odd numbers? How about when you add one odd and one even number? Are you more likely to get cards whose sums are odd or even when you play this game? What if the game were based on picking up odd sums? Would it be harder to win if you could only pick up odd sums?

Pyramid 10

Materials

- 1 deck of cards, with face cards removed

Instructions

Two partners play against the deck. The object of the game is to pick up the entire pyramid as you go through the deck once.

1. Shuffle the deck, and arrange twenty-one cards in a pyramid, as shown below:

2. Put the rest of the deck face down next to the pyramid.

3. Note "free cards": A free card is one that has no other card overlapping it. When the game begins, only the six cards on the pyramid's bottom row qualify as free.

4. Remove all free 10s *and* pairs of cards that add up to ten. Set these aside. These cards are now completely out of play.

5. Continue removing free 10s and pairs adding up to ten until there are no more possibilities to be picked up.

6. Turn over one card from the deck. If it's a 10 or can combine to make ten with a free card from the pyramid, set these cards aside. If you *can't* use the card you've turned up, set it face up below the pyramid. You may be able to use it later.

7. Turn up another card. Follow the same instructions as in Step 6. Each time you are able to remove cards from the pyramid by turning over a new card, see if this top card is now usable with the free cards in the pyramid.

8. The game ends when you've turned over all the cards in the deck and you can't make and remove any more totals of ten.

Note: Children may need help with building the pyramid correctly, so demonstrate this aspect of the game carefully. After the rules of the game have been established and you are modeling playing the game, ask, "What numbers would we like to turn over next?" This question focuses the children's attention on the combinations of ten. (If there's a free 8, then we would hope for a 2 to be turned over.) This kind of question also draws children into the game's mathematics. You might want to follow up with a statement like, "Pyramid Ten is a fun game that helps us get to know all the combinations for 10. That's why we play it during math time." By being explicit about your reason for choosing activities, you reinforce math learning and add a sense of purpose to a playful experience.

The following game was also devised by a second grader (see *Math by All Means: Probability, Grades 1–2* [Tank 1996]).

1 to 10

Materials

- 2 dice
- 1 deck of cards, with face cards removed

Instructions

The object of the game is to get rid of all your cards. One player gets all the red cards. The other gets all the black cards.

1. Player 1: Roll the dice and find the sum of the two numbers. Discard any set of your cards that have the same sum as the dice. For example, suppose you rolled a five and a three. That adds up to eight. You can make eight many ways: 5 + 3, or 4 + 4, or 6 + 1 + 1. Choose one way to make the sum, then discard those cards.

2. Player 1: If you can't make the first sum with the cards you have, roll again. If you can't make this new sum, roll again. If you can't make this third sum, you automatically lose.

3. Players 1 and 2: Take turns rolling the dice and discarding cards.

4. The first player to get rid of all his or her cards is the winner.

Chapter 3

October/ November

DEVELOPING PLACE VALUE UNDERSTANDING

The Learning Environment

Your class is probably beginning to settle in, with students getting to know one another and starting to understand your expectations. The math focus this month will be on helping the children gain confidence and skill in understanding underlying assumptions about our number system. As you work with your students this month, try to resist the temptation to teach rote procedures. The payoff will come when you notice your students beginning to devise their own methods of finding correct answers and feeling more competent as mathematicians. ■

During the fall months, you will:

- introduce the big ideas required for developing number sense with large numbers.
- let your students know how interested and confident you are in their thinking.
- reinforce the notion that making mistakes is part of the learning process.
- encourage persistence in all of your students.
- pay careful attention to how second graders think about number concepts by having them talk and write about their problem solving.
- focus on how each child is progressing individually.
- give yourself permission to have bad days but learn from your mistakes by analyzing what went wrong and why.

The Mathematics

This month's math activities will give your second graders continued opportunities to make use of the single-digit number facts. They'll play more number games and think through strategies for becoming confident and efficient when adding single-digit numbers.

Much of the fall will also be spent developing number sense for large numbers. Second-grade curriculum often asks students to add and subtract large numbers early in the year, long before they have had a chance to develop understanding about the underlying structure of our base-10 number system. To avoid the mathematical confusion that develops in children's minds when they are asked to use rote procedures for which they have little or no understanding, the fall months will be spent playing games, doing activities, and solving problems that lead to developing place value understanding. By the *end of the year*, second graders can have a robust sense of number that allows them to add and subtract multi-digit numbers with the same efficiency and confidence they have for smaller numbers.

During October and November, students should do games and activities that give them opportunities to:

- get to know the number 10, inside and out.
- learn all the doubles (1 + 1 through 10 + 10).
- begin to develop strategies for all the single-digit number facts.
- count and group by 2s, 5s, and 10s.
- solve word problems with answers less than 100.

In the spring, you'll once again focus on number, with addition and subtraction as the main priority. Students will have a chance to learn important concepts in the fall, "sleep on them" during the winter months, and then return to them in the spring when most of them have taken a big jump in their cognitive maturity.

The activities described in this chapter serve as examples of ways to convey these mathematical ideas. Some lessons are presented in detail, to help you think through how to present a lesson. Use what you learn from these lessons to decide how to get the most mathematics out of other similar lessons. You'll likely find that you need to augment these lessons with additional activities of your own choosing (see the Professional Resources section of the References at the back of this book). By augmenting in these ways, you can put together a complete curriculum that works for your students and your teaching situation.

Today's Number and Calendar Making

Continue the daily routine of *Today's Number*. But introduce the ideas listed below as you touch on each of these concepts during math:

- Use combinations of ten (5 + 5, 6 + 4, 1 + 2 + 3 + 4) in equations today. (Encourage students to generate these combinations as a group before you present this rule.)
- Use doubles in equations today.
- Use both addition and subtraction.
- Use multiples of five today (or two, or ten). (If the rule is *use multiples of five*, take a moment to count by fives with your class to remind them what you mean by *multiples of five*.)

When you gather students together to share equations, discuss the use of fact families and the commutative and associative properties. For instance, if someone offers 40 − 10 = 30, first see if anyone suggests that you could "prove" the equation by noting that 30 + 10 = 40. If none of your students makes this suggestion, then introduce the idea yourself. Similarly, if equations come up that illustrate the commutative property, point out that with any addition the addends' order is unimportant. For example, one child might suggest 10 + 2 + 8 = 20, then another may suggest 8 + 2 + 10 = 20.

Set aside some time early in the month to go over the important classroom events for each of these two months, giving the children time to make their calendars to take home.

Getting to Know the Number 10

Our number system is based on groupings of ten, so it's essential that students become familiar with the number. They need to be able to take it apart and put it back together again with ease. The following activities can help them master those skills.

Number Games with Two Addends

Pyramid 10

Use the *Pyramid 10* game described in Chapter 2 to give your students practice with number combinations that add up to ten. Encourage students to play this and other games based on combinations of ten often.

Tens Go Fish

Play a version of the traditional game *Go Fish* that is presented in the book *Coins, Coupons, and Combinations* (Economopoulos 1997). In *Tens Go Fish*, players are each dealt five cards from a deck that has had the face cards and the 10s removed. Taking turns, players put aside pairs of cards that add up to ten. Play continues until all the cards in the deck are used up, at which point each person writes out the sums of ten he or she has put aside.

To keep play moving, Player 1 first puts aside any two cards in hand that add to ten. He replaces the pairs he was able to put aside by picking up *two* new cards from the deck for every pair he puts aside. It's OK to keep picking up new cards to replace any new combinations in hand that add up to ten and are put aside. Once Player 1 puts aside all his possible pairs that add up to ten (or determines that he does not have any pairs that do so), he can go on a "fishing expedition" by asking his partner for a specific card from that player's hand.

If the fishing expedition enables him to acquire a card that can make ten, he puts the pair down and takes *one* card from the top of the deck. If this new card mates to make another ten, he puts that pair down and picks up another card (and so on) before play passes to Player 2.

If the fishing expedition is unsuccessful, play passes to Player 2.

The end of this game is nicely anticlimactic. There's no fuss made about how many pairs of ten each player has acquired. Instead, the focus remains on the math. Each player is asked to list his or her combinations that add to ten, before choosing a new game to play or playing another round of the same game.

Games for Decomposing 10

The following four activities can help students break ten into more than two addends:

Sweet 13

Modify the *Sweet 13* game, described in Chapter 2, to become *Sweet 10*. Simply change the target number from thirteen to ten. This shift will give students opportunities to use two *or more* addends to get to ten.

Individual Books About 10

Once you've introduced the notion of using more than two addends in an equation, assign students the task of making their own personal list of equations for ten using three addends. On another day, invite them to make a list of equations for ten using four addends—on up to using ten addends. When each child arranges these lists in order from the least number of addends possible to the most, he or she will have an impressive book about 10. When you assign this activity, make sure students have access to counters while they work out their equations. (See Figures 3–1 and 3–2.)

3 Numbers

$$1 + 1 + 8 = 10$$
$$1 + 2 + 7 = 10$$
$$2 + 2 + 6 = 10$$
$$2 + 3 + 5 = 10$$
$$3 + 3 + 4 = 10$$
$$3 + 4 + 3 = 10$$
$$4 + 4 + 2 = 10$$
$$5 + 4 + 1 = 10$$

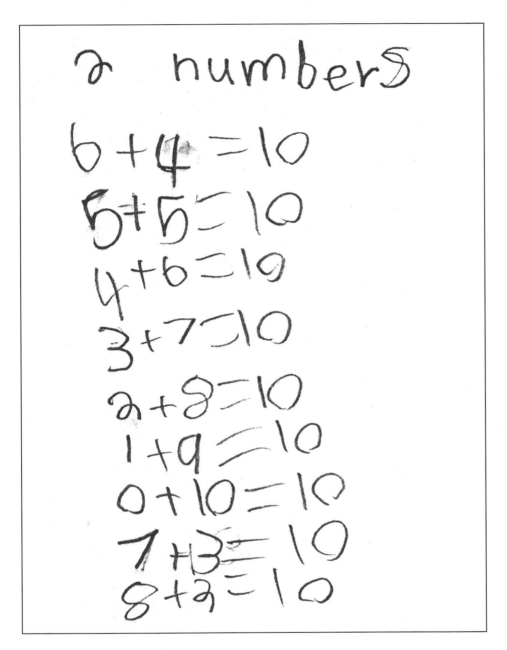

FIGURE 3–2 ◀

Alan found almost all the ways to make 10 using two numbers.

Memory

The old *Memory* game can be modified to give students numeric practice. Come up with a name for it that you and your students like. Instead of looking for two cards that look the same, the students will look for sets of cards that add up to ten. Here's how it works:

1. Remove the face cards and 10s from a deck of cards.

2. Arrange fours rows of five cards each, face side down.

3. Set the deck aside, also face down.

4. Players take turns turning over cards, looking for sums of ten. It's OK to keep overturning cards, as long as the total is less than ten. For instance, if a player turns over a 3 and then a 4, the sum so far is only 7, so he or she can turn over yet another card. Once a player's total goes over ten, her turn is over.

5. Players may pick up any sets of cards that total ten exactly and put them aside in a pile (so they don't get mixed up with other sets of ten). Cards that are used are replaced from the deck, and then the next player gets a turn.

6. When no more sets of ten can be made, each player lists the combinations for ten that he or she set aside.

10 for Dinner

The children's literature book *10 for Dinner*, by Jo Ellen Bogart, is the perfect stepping-off point for decomposing ten into smaller numbers. This resource also gives students opportunities to practice expressing a mathematical concept in a format that's familiar to them. They get to draw a picture that depicts a combination of ten.

In *10 for Dinner,* ten active young people are invited to Margo's birthday party. Here's how to use the story:

1. Read the book to your class for the pleasure of the story itself.

2. Then read it a second time, noting the equations you could write for each new situation. For example, ask, "How could we use numbers that reflect the different games Margo's guests want to play? On pages fourteen and fifteen, we learn that [and you might want to write this on the chalkboard]:

   one guest said 'jump rope,'

   four said 'tag,'

   four said 'hide and seek,'

   but one guest said 'dirty-double no-hands blindfolded marbles.'

   We can use the equation one plus four plus four plus one equals ten [1 + 4 + 4 + 1 = 10] to tell about the different choices."

3. After going through all the possible ways to make ten that are depicted in the book, suggest that you can make a class book modeled on *10 for Dinner*. Start by exploring situations that could reasonably involve ten people. For example, ten people might be in a line at a movie theater. How could they be sorted? Maybe by what they're wearing. What might that look like? (Possibly three people are wearing sweatsuits, two are wearing shorts, and five are wearing blue jeans.) Or maybe they could be sorted by their ages (four adults, two teenagers, and two

young children). Or ten children might be playing at a park. They might be grouped by the equipment they're playing on, though your students might have other ideas. Have an open-ended conversation about these possibilities to get children thinking about possibilities for when they begin to work on their own page for the book. You'll also send the message that you value your students' thinking

4. When you have the sense that the children are ready to work independently, ask them to think quietly for a moment about what setting they will put their ten people in and how they will sort them into groups to form their equations. Ask for volunteers to share their ideas, then respond enthusiastically.

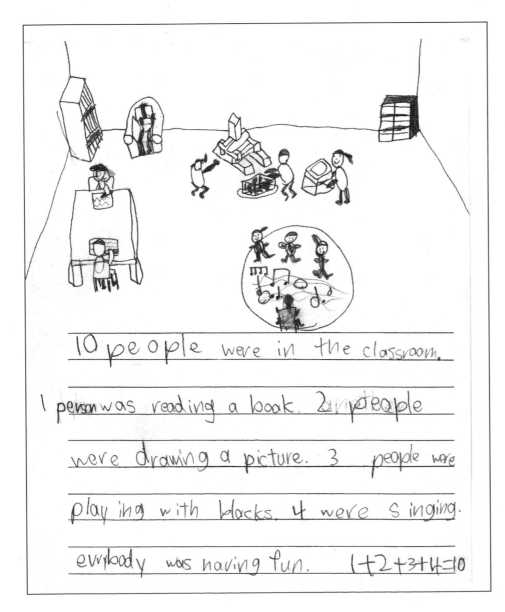

10 people were in the classroom.

1 person was reading a book. 2 people were drawing a picture. 3 people were playing with blocks. 4 were singing. evrybody was having fun.   1+2+3+4=10

FIGURE 3–3 ◄

Edwin chose a classroom setting and enjoyed showing
1 + 2 + 3 + 4 = 10.

FIGURE 3–4   ▶

**Corie chose one of her
favorite places, the
school library.**

10 People were at the library. 2 of
them were checking out books. 2 of
them were reading books. 5 Of them were
listining to a story. 1 of them was reading
to the 5 People. 2+2+5+1=10

5. Pass out paper that has space for both a picture and writing. Ask the children to draw their ten people, write about how they are sorted into smaller groups, and include an equation for ten that reflects the way the people are grouped. Then compile the finished pages into a class book, share it with your students during a group story time, and make it available for individuals to read during independent reading time. (See Figures 3–3 [on page 53], 3–4, and 3–5.)

FIGURE 3–5 ◀

Selby broke ten down into a series of twos.

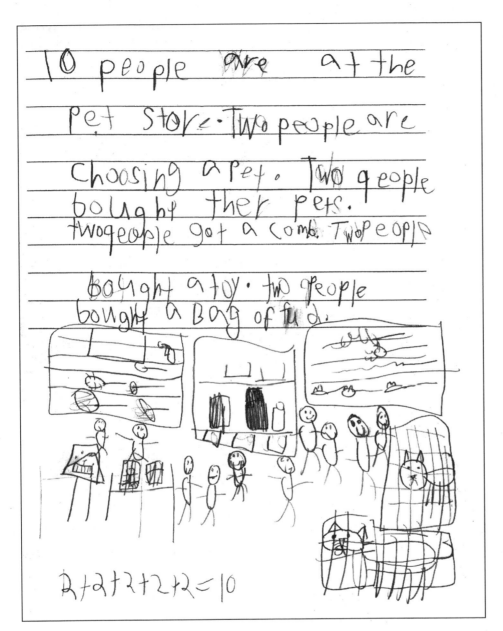

10 people are at the pet store. Two people are choosing a pet. Two geople bought ther pets. two geople got a comb. Two peopl bought a toy. two geople bought a Bag of fud.

2+2+2+2+2=10

Doubles

Memorizing the doubles (1 +1, 2 + 2, 3 + 3 . . . 10 + 10) seems to come easily for most children, especially if they're allowed to draw on real-world mathematics. Once students know the doubles, they can start to think about the near doubles. For instance, if you know that 6 + 6 = 12, it's an easy step to 6 + 7 = 13. This kind of thinking, in turn, leads to the notion that we can develop strategies, based on number relationships, for mastering all of the number facts. Memorization can fade into the background as thinking and reasoning take over.

Here's some fun ways to get to know doubles.

Real-Life Doubles

With your class, make a chart based on doubles in the real world. Start with the doubles shown below, and encourage students to add ideas:

1 + 1 = a pair of shoes

2 + 2 = the wheels on a wagon (two in front and two in back)

3 + 3 = sodas in a six-pack, three on each side

4 + 4 = the fingers on two hands, thumbs turned under

5 + 5 = the toes on two feet

6 + 6 = a dozen eggs in a carton, six in each row

7 + 7 = the first two weeks in February, or Valentine's Day

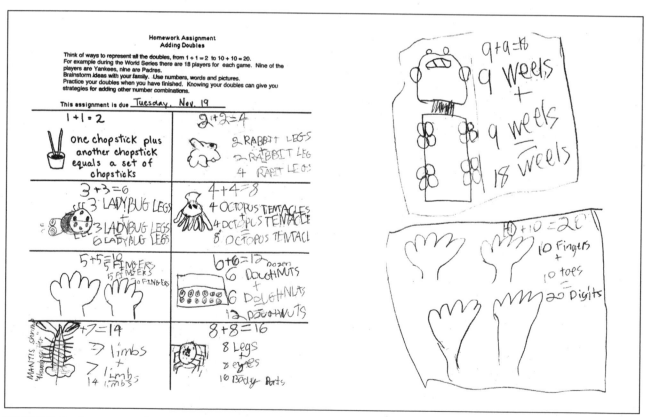

FIGURE 3–6 ▲

Corie found ways to illustrate all the doubles.

8 + 8 = a sixteen-pack of crayons, divided in two rows

9 + 9 = two baseball teams, one in the field and one up to bat

Children can get involved in learning doubles by observing items they see every day, at home and in the classroom, and recording them on a chart. (See Figure 3–6 and Blackline Masters.)

Monster Body Parts

Introduce this activity by reading and enjoying the illustrations in a book such as *My Monster Mama Loves Me So* by Laura Leuck, illustrations by Mark Buehner. In this book, it's not unusual for a monster to have only two toes on each foot, or three arms on each side of his body. Each child can decide how many toes (or arms or antenna or fingers) to draw to illustrate the notion of a double. Make sure students write equations showing which double the monster illustrates. You may want to place limits on the numbers, to help the children stay focused on the doubles 1 + 1 through 10 + 10. Consider compiling a class book to which each child contributes one page. Or, have each child make his or her own book in which he or she illustrates several doubles. (See Figures 3–7 and 3–8.)

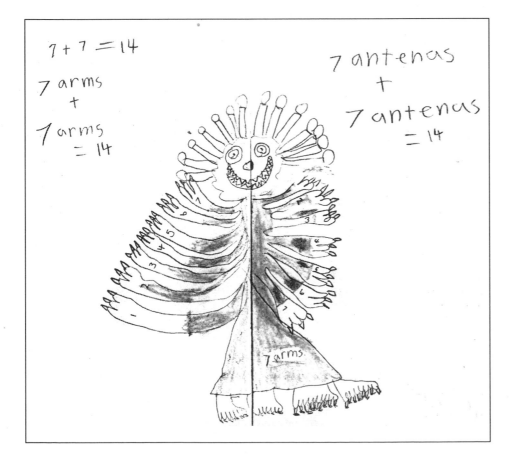

FIGURE 3–7 ◄

Oksana's double monster is exuberant.

FIGURE 3–8   ▶

Jason's double monster for fourteen is understated.

Two of Everything

The book *Two of Everything*, by Lily Toy Hong, tells of a magic pot that doubles anything that falls into it. Have your students write story problems that use this situation. Here's an example: "If five pumpkins got pushed into the magic pot, how many pumpkins would you take out?" Students can write the problem on the front of a sheet of paper, then draw a picture and equation on the back that illustrate the answer. Gather these pages to make a *Two of Everything* class book. (See Figures 3–9 and 3–10.)

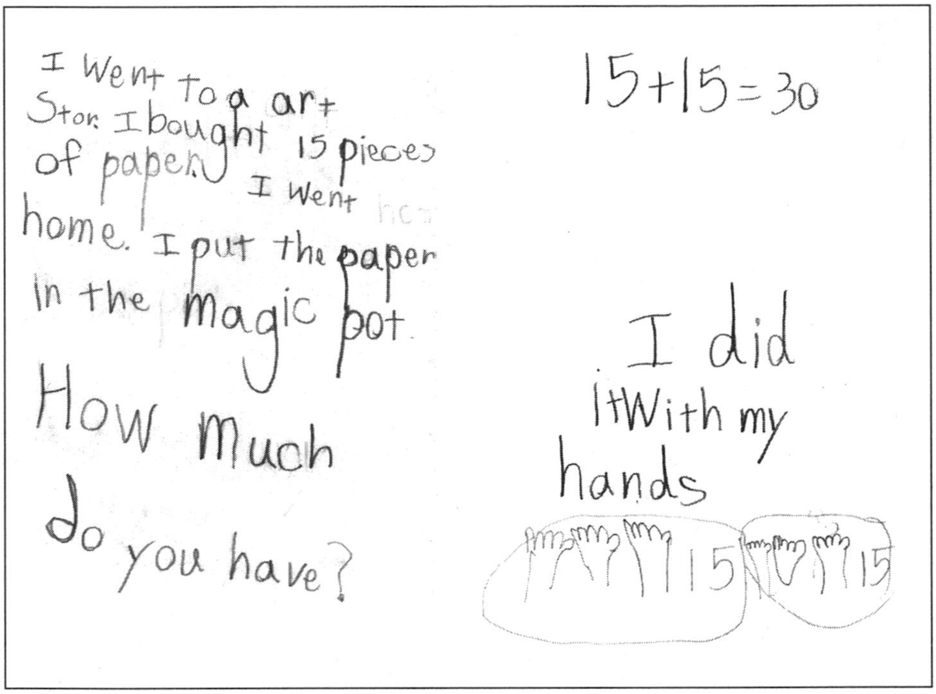

I Went to a art Stor. I bought 15 pieces of paper. I Went home. I put the paper in the magic pot. How much do you have?

$15 + 15 = 30$

I did It With my hands

FIGURE 3-9 ◄

Daniel wrote his story problem and then showed how he used his fingers to solve 15 + 15.

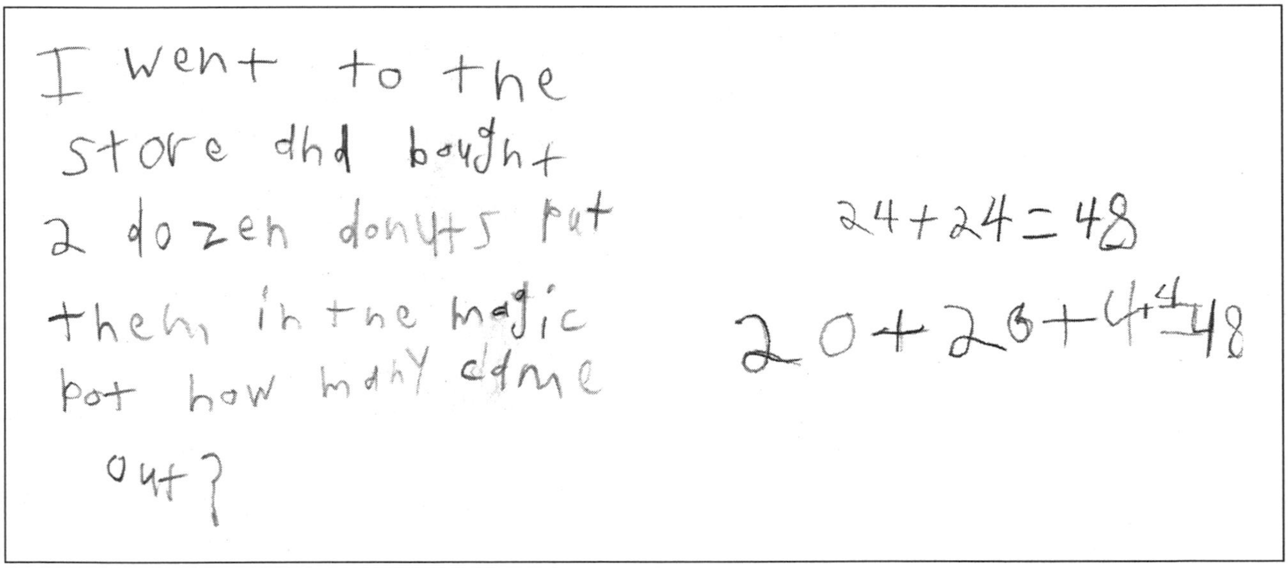

I Went to the store dhd bought 2 dozen donyts put them in the magic pot how mdhy cdme out?

$24 + 24 = 48$

$20 + 20 + 4 + 4 = 48$

FIGURE 3-10 ▲

Benjamin used important understandings about decomposing numbers to solve his problem.

Number-Facts Strategies

Having strategies for easy and quick recall of the 121 basic addition facts, 0 + 0 through 10 + 10, is essential for mathematical competency. Since you want students to be in control of these basic facts, avoid situations that take control away from them. Timed tests may seem to encourage competency until you recall the stomach-wrenching feelings they engender in so many children. It's hard for any of us to remain in control when we feel under attack. So no matter how much you want your students to know their facts, don't create a situation that spawns anxiety and a feeling of incompetence within your children.

The following series of discussions are designed to help your students feel and be more in control of the basic facts (Tank 1996). In addition, these lessons give you a chance to see the effect of all the practice your students have been getting throughout the fall, as they've used the single-digit addition facts to play games.

1. Get ready by displaying the facts 0 + 0 through 10 + 10 in an organized way. You can make a chart like the one below (see Figure 3–11), write the facts on the board, or use a large pocket chart to display the individual facts, one fact per pocket. If you use a pocket chart, have transparent plastic squares the same size as the display cards, so that you can highlight facts as you discuss them.

2. During the first discussion, present the chart to your students. After they've oohed and ahhed at the size of the chart, ask them to estimate how many different facts there are. After hearing their estimates, tell them that there are a total of 121 facts and that eventually they will know them all.

3. To help your students get over the shock of the sheer number of facts, let them see that they already know many of the facts. Ask, "Are there any facts that you think most kindergartners know?" Your students will likely point out examples such as 0 + 0, 6 + 1, and 2 + 2, facts that are found in the first three rows and columns. (Kindergartners, in fact, may not know about adding zero to any number, but most second graders do. What you're really looking for here are the combinations that most second graders know. By couching the question in terms of kindergartners, your students are less likely to become competitive with one another. Instead, they'll focus on which combinations are generally easy to know.)

4. For the plus zero, plus one, and plus two facts, many second graders use a simple *counting on* strategy. Take a moment to discuss this strategy with your students. Say something like, "To figure out six plus

0+0	1+0	2+0	3+0	4+0	5+0	6+0	7+0	8+0	9+0	10+0
0+1	1+1	2+1	3+1	4+1	5+1	6+1	7+1	8+1	9+1	10+1
0+2	1+2	2+2	3+2	4+2	5+2	6+2	7+2	8+2	9+2	10+2
0+3	1+3	2+3	3+3	4+3	5+3	6+3	7+3	8+3	9+3	10+3
0+4	1+4	2+4	3+4	4+4	5+4	6+4	7+4	8+4	9+4	10+4
0+5	1+5	2+5	3+5	4+5	5+5	6+5	7+5	8+5	9+5	10+5
0+6	1+6	2+6	3+6	4+6	5+6	6+6	7+6	8+6	9+6	10+6
0+7	1+7	2+7	3+7	4+7	5+7	6+7	7+7	8+7	9+7	10+7
0+8	1+8	2+8	3+8	4+8	5+8	6+8	7+8	8+8	9+8	10+8
0+9	1+9	2+9	3+9	4+9	5+9	6+9	7+9	8+9	9+9	10+9
0+10	1+10	2+10	3+10	1+10	1+10	6+10	7+10	8+10	9+10	10+10

FIGURE 3–11 ◀

A chart displaying 0 + 0 through 10 + 10 in an organized way.

two, it's easy to count up two more from six. You can just say, 'six [pause], seven, eight.' Who has a way to use the counting on strategy for seven plus two?" You'll now be able to circle or highlight the first three rows and the first three columns of basic facts. Note you've narrowed the field by fifty-nine facts, leaving only sixty-four. (See Figure 3–12.)

5. End the day's discussion by explaining that in the days to come, you'll be thinking about strategies that work for the other sixty-four facts.

0+0	1+0	2+0	3+0	4+0	5+0	6+0	7+0	8+0	9+0	10+0
0+1	1+1	2+1	3+1	4+1	5+1	6+1	7+1	8+1	9+1	10+1
0+2	1+2	2+2	3+2	4+2	5+2	6+2	7+2	8+2	9+2	10+2
0+3	1+3	2+3	3+3	4+3	5+3	6+3	7+3	8+3	9+3	10+3
0+4	1+4	2+4	3+4	4+4	5+4	6+4	7+4	8+4	9+4	10+4
0+5	1+5	2+5	3+5	4+5	5+5	6+5	7+5	8+5	9+5	10+5
0+6	1+6	2+6	3+6	4+6	5+6	6+6	7+6	8+6	9+6	10+6
0+7	1+7	2+7	3+7	4+7	5+7	6+7	7+7	8+7	9+7	10+7
0+8	1+8	2+8	3+8	4+8	5+8	6+8	7+8	8+8	9+8	10+8
0+9	1+9	2+9	3+9	4+9	5+9	6+9	7+9	8+9	9+9	10+9
0+10	1+10	2+10	3+10	1+10	1+10	6+10	7+10	8+10	9+10	10+10

FIGURE 3–12 ◀

Students show what they know by highlighting the chart.

6. On another day, look at the doubles and notice the diagonal they make on the chart. (See Figure 3–13.) Explain that if the students haven't memorized any of these facts, they need to start working on them now. This might be a good time to introduce the notion of taking home a fact in your pocket (or in your shoe). Arrange for a time when students can write down any of the doubles they don't know on a small slip of paper. They can then each choose one to put into a pocket and study, until they can easily recall it.

7. At another time, look at the near doubles, (5 + 4, 6 + 5, and so on) on either side of the doubles. (See Figure 3–14.) Talk about strategies for learning these combinations. Don't be surprised if some children still need to use counting. Other students will reason that if 6 + 6 = 12, then 7 + 6 must equal 13. The big idea here is for students to articulate strategies that work for them.

   I sometimes explain to my students that whenever I'm confronted with the combination 8 + 9, I first think 8 + 8 = 16. Then I quickly move on to 8 + 9 = 17. It's important for children to know that these kinds of strategies are legitimate and that each child needs to figure out what helps *him* or *her* become proficient with the combinations.

8. On another day, give students time to write down their strategies for a problem such as 7 + 4, one fact that they have not yet discussed. Have the youngsters share these strategies with one another. They'll remain focused on developing strategies that have meaning for individual students.

FIGURE 3–13　▶

Using the chart to show doubles.

0+0	1+0	2+0	3+0	4+0	5+0	6+0	7+0	8+0	9+0	10+0
0+1	1+1	2+1	3+1	4+1	5+1	6+1	7+1	8+1	9+1	10+1
0+2	1+2	2+2	3+2	4+2	5+2	6+2	7+2	8+2	9+2	10+2
0+3	1+3	2+3	3+3	4+3	5+3	6+3	7+3	8+3	9+3	10+3
0+4	1+4	2+4	3+4	4+4	5+4	6+4	7+4	8+4	9+4	10+4
0+5	1+5	2+5	3+5	4+5	5+5	6+5	7+5	8+5	9+5	10+5
0+6	1+6	2+6	3+6	4+6	5+6	6+6	7+6	8+6	9+6	10+6
0+7	1+7	2+7	3+7	4+7	5+7	6+7	7+7	8+7	9+7	10+7
0+8	1+8	2+8	3+8	4+8	5+8	6+8	7+8	8+8	9+8	10+8
0+9	1+9	2+9	3+9	4+9	5+9	6+9	7+9	8+9	9+9	10+9
0+10	1+10	2+10	3+10	1+10	1+10	6+10	7+10	8+10	9+10	10+10

FIGURE 3-14 ◄

Using the chart to show near doubles.

0+0	1+0	2+0	3+0	4+0	5+0	6+0	7+0	8+0	9+0	10+0
0+1	1+1	2+1	3+1	4+1	5+1	6+1	7+1	8+1	9+1	10+1
0+2	1+2	2+2	3+2	4+2	5+2	6+2	7+2	8+2	9+2	10+2
0+3	1+3	2+3	3+3	(4+3)	5+3	6+3	7+3	8+3	9+3	10+3
0+4	1+4	2+4	(3+4)	4+4	(5+4)	6+4	7+4	8+4	9+4	10+4
0+5	1+5	2+5	3+5	(4+5)	5+5	(6+5)	7+5	8+5	9+5	10+5
0+6	1+6	2+6	3+6	4+6	(5+6)	6+6	(7+6)	8+6	9+6	10+6
0+7	1+7	2+7	3+7	4+7	5+7	(6+7)	7+7	(8+7)	9+7	10+7
0+8	1+8	2+8	3+8	4+8	5+8	6+8	(7+8)	8+8	(9+8)	10+8
0+9	1+9	2+9	3+9	4+9	5+9	6+9	7+9	(8+9)	9+9	(10+9)
0+10	1+10	2+10	3+10	1+10	1+10	6+10	7+10	8+10	(9+10)	10+10

9. Eventually, draw students' attention to the strategy of adding 10 to any number to systematically eliminate another block of facts. Some children may be able to piggyback on the +10 idea and see that if 6 + 10 = 16 then 6 + 9 = 15. Understanding that relationship enables some children to eliminate yet another row of facts.

As you go through this process, be realistic. Just because you've taken the time to discuss these strategies, not all your second graders will be mature enough to learn all the math facts even by the end of the school year. The important thing is that they continue to have experiences that encourage them to use number combinations so they build competence over time. My husband, an accountant who owns a small business specializing in tax preparation, tells the story of how his well-meaning second-grade teacher made him wear mittens because she caught him counting on his fingers when doing math. He explains that the mittens were actually a great help: While wearing them, he could move his fingers to keep track of his count without getting caught by his teacher! You'll be relieved (for his clients' sake) to know that my husband did eventually learn all of his math facts. He just needed time—and his fingers—to become fully competent. Figure 3–15 is a helpful schematic showing number-facts strategies for addition.

Homework

One way to encourage students to develop strategies for learning the combinations—and to let parents know about your class's efforts—is to send home the assignment shown on page 65. (See Blackline Masters.)

1. ADDING 0, 1, 2, OR 3:
   DOUBLES STRATEGY

0	0	0	0	0	0	0	0	0	0	0
+0	+1	+2	+3	+4	+5	+6	+7	+8	+9	+10

1	2	3	4	5	6	7	8	9	10
+0	+0	+0	+0	+0	+0	+0	+0	+0	+0

1	1	1	1	1	1	1	1	1	1
+1	+2	+3	+4	+5	+6	+7	+8	+9	+10

2	3	4	5	6	7	8	9	10
+1	+1	+1	+1	+1	+1	+1	+1	+1

2	2	2	2	2	2	2	2	2
+2	+3	+4	+5	+6	+7	+8	+9	+10

3	4	5	6	7	8	9	10
+2	+2	+2	+2	+2	+2	+2	+2

3	3	3	3	3	3	3	3
+3	+4	+5	+6	+7	+8	+9	+10

4	5	6	7	8	9	10
+3	+3	+3	+3	+3	+3	+3

2. ADDING A NUMBER TO ITSELF:
   DOUBLES STRATEGY

4	5	6	7	8	9
+4	+5	+6	+7	+8	+9

ADDING NEAR DOUBLES:
DOUBLE PLUS ONE STRATEGY

4	5	5	6	6	7	7	8	8	9
+5	+4	+6	+5	+7	+6	+8	+7	+9	+8

3. ADDING NINE:
   PATTERN FOR ADDING NINE STRATEGY

9	4	9	5	9	6	9	7
+4	+9	+5	+9	+6	+9	+7	+9

4. ADDING TEN:
   PATTERN FOR ADDING TEN STRATEGY

10	4	10	5	10	6	10	7	10	8	10	9
+4	+10	+5	+10	+6	+10	+7	+10	+8	+10	+9	+10

5. THE REMAINING FACTS

4	6	4	7	4	8	5	7	5	8	6	8
+6	+4	+7	+4	+0	+4	+7	+5	+8	+5	+8	+6

FIGURE 3–15   ▲

A schematic showing number-facts strategies for addition.

Single-Digit Addition

Make sure you know your doubles. If you don't, practice them every day.

1 + 1   2 + 2   3 + 3   4 + 4   5 + 5   6 + 6   7 + 7   8 + 8   9 + 9   10 + 10

In class we looked at the chart for addition facts from 0 + 0 through 10 + 10. There were 121 facts! That's a lot.

When we looked at the chart closely, we discovered that there were many facts that everyone already knew, so we crossed those out.

The facts listed below are the ones that you may still need to practice. The important thing is to have strategies that make sense to you so you can quickly find the answers when you need them.

4 + 3	5 + 3	6 + 3	7 + 3	8 + 3	9 + 3
	5 + 4	6 + 4	7 + 4	8 + 4	9 + 4
		6 + 5	7 + 5	8 + 5	9 + 5
			7 + 6	8 + 6	9 + 6
				8 + 7	9 + 7
					9 + 8

Each day, choose three or more of these addition facts. Write your strategies for getting the answer to each fact on a separate piece of paper.

Note to parents: The purpose of this assignment is to encourage children to use their number sense (especially the ability to decompose numbers and knowledge about how numbers relate to one another) to develop strategies for efficiently doing single digit addition. Different children may come up with different strategies to solve the same problem—the important thing is for each child to think about what works for him or her.

Memorization is less important than having a quick and accurate way of coming up with the answer. For instance, when I want to answer 8 + 9, I say, "8 + 8 = 16 so 8 + 9 = 17." I can do this in the blink of an eye. In class we're talking about the kinds of strategies that make us mathematically powerful. Your child should have many ideas to draw on. You might want to share some of your own strategies with your child. Just remember that your child may go about solving the problems differently, and that's fine. We must construct understanding and methods that work for each one of us.

Larger Numbers

To get a feel for why place value can be daunting to young children, consider the number 52. What does it take for a person to understand what those symbols represent? Here are some possibilities:

- Students need to know that the *position* of each digit is significant. For instance, 25 does not represent the same quantity as 52. This is obvious to adults, but not so obvious to young children, who may still be unclear about directionality.

- They need to know that the 5 is in the 10s place and the 2 is in the 1s place. Thus they need a feel for the base-10 nature of our number system.

- Youngsters must know how to multiply 5 by 10 to get 50 and 2 by 1 to get 2. These understandings get at the multiplicative nature of our number system.

- Children also need to be able to add 50 and 2 to get 52. This gets at the additive nature of our number system and indicates that you can decompose numbers and put them back together again.

- To really grasp what 52 represents as a quantity, kids also must know how that number relates to other numbers. For example, 52 is closer to 50 than to 60, about half as much as 100, and a little more than double 25. That's having a feel for the relative magnitude of 52.

What a lot to understand—and the concepts grow even more complicated when you add 52 to another number! Equally important, your goal is to teach these ideas in such a way that students learn not only to add and subtract confidently, but also to develop a positive attitude toward mathematics. Only then can they tackle more difficult math concepts, from fractions to algebra, in future grades. Luckily, second graders are willing and eager to learn about the number system—if you present the concepts in the form of engaging games and activities that make sense to their young minds.

Counting and Grouping

Your students probably know the rote sequence for counting by 10s. But because they are used to the "one more than" relationship based on counting by 1s, they may have little understanding of the quantities that sequence represents. The following activities give your students firsthand experience for understanding the 10s and 1s components of our number system.

Handfuls

Encourage your students to count the same group of objects (in quantities more than twenty but less than 100) in different ways (by 1s, 2s, 5s, 10s, etc.) Young children enjoy counting, so you don't have to go to elaborate lengths to create situations that will intrigue them. You can prepare bags filled with cubes, or just have the children take handfuls of objects and then count how many they've scooped up.

A lesson could follow this format, in which you ask some or all of the questions suggested in the steps below, depending on how focused your students are during classroom discussions. Teaching is an art, not a prescription, and you have to judge what's right for your students on any given day. Here are the steps:

1. Gather your students in a circle. Have a tub of cubes close at hand. Say, "I'm going to take as many cubes as I can with both my right hand and my left hand. Who has an idea of how many cubes I might be able to scoop up? Think about your answer for a moment and then write your idea on the palm of your hand, using the pointer finger of your other hand. That way, you'll have an invisible answer that you can change as you get more information."

2. Give students a moment to think, and then ask for volunteers who want to share their estimates. As students give answers, ask them to explain their reasoning. You might get suggestions that range from, "That's just what I think," to "Well, you'll probably be able to grab ten in each hand, and I know that ten plus ten equals twenty."

3. Thank the students who have offered possibilities. Then say, "We can get a better idea of the amount if we have a little more information. I'm going to take one handful. Then we'll count the cubes and see if that helps us make an estimation."

   Do the scooping with one hand. Then count the cubes one by one, asking your students to count along with you. Let's assume you were able to scoop up about fourteen cubes.

4. Now pose a slightly different estimation question. Ask, "When I add my other handful to this group, do you think there will be more than twenty cubes altogether, or fewer than twenty cubes?" Asking for an estimate in this way encourages children to think about the relative magnitude of numbers (how numbers compare to one another). It also frees them up to think in terms of an estimate, rather than an exact number. It helps them become flexible in their thinking about numbers—a major goal for this time of year.

5. Give the children time to record their invisible answer to this new question. Then ask for volunteers to share their thinking about how they answered the question. Remind them that you don't want an exact number this time, but point out that you are still very interested in their thinking.

6. Now count the number of cubes. Start with the number that represented your first handful, count on to reach a total for the two

handfuls. Say, "When we counted all of the cubes I could scoop with my two hands, we got a total of twenty-seven. Is that more than twenty or fewer than twenty?" Ask for volunteers to explain their thinking. Move on to talking about what your students will be doing for the rest of the period.

Here's how you can build on the preceding process:

1. Ask, "If we counted all of my cubes in a different way, say by twos, how many do you think there would be? Write your answer on the palm of your hand." This is an obvious answer for adults and even for some second graders. Yet it is not obvious to all second graders—especially as the totals get larger. You can have volunteers answer this question or just let it be a rhetorical query, designed to encourage an internal monologue within students' minds.

2. Have students recount the cubes out loud with you, this time moving two cubes aside as you count by 2s.

3. Explain that students will now work with partners on the handfuls activity. Since they will be working in pairs, they'll end up with a total of four handfuls to count. Remind them that they need to first estimate if they'll have more than or fewer than twenty cubes when they put all four handfuls together. Then explain that they'll need to count the total number of cubes in at least two different ways.
   On the chalkboard, write the following:

   Handfuls
       We estimated that we would get (*more/less*) than 20 cubes.
       We counted by 2s and got _____ cubes.
       We counted by 5s and got _____ cubes.
       Our total is (*more/less*) than 20 cubes.

4. Pass out plain pieces of paper and explain that students can use the same format shown on the chalkboard to report their findings. They don't need to use the exact wording that's on the board, but they should include all of the above information on their paper, including their name and the date.

5. Explain that the children can repeat the activity if they complete their first handful paper before the period is over. Muse out loud, "I wonder if you'll get exactly the same number of cubes the second time you do Handfuls?" End the directed part of the lesson by reminding the class that this is a business-talk-only time. Note that you're looking forward to seeing the results of their work.

6. Have the children return to their desks and begin working. Circulate, showing interest in how your students are accomplishing the task. Take a few moments to observe the whole class for a moment, noting who might be having trouble getting started. Go to those tables first. With an even tone, ask a question such as, "What do you and your partner need to do first?" This kind of gentle nudging lets students know that you expect them to get on with the mathematics. The fact that you're nearby may be all they need to get started. Continue circulating among the children as they work.

A nice follow-up activity to *Handfuls* is to record the totals that all the groups got at the end of the lesson and look at the range of totals.

Estimating 20

To further encourage estimating and counting, suggest a target number of items for each student to try to pick up with one hand. Twenty is a good choice for this time of year. Have beans, macaroni, buttons, etc. in jars or bags that a child's hand will fit into comfortably. Here's how it works:

1. Model the scooping and estimating by saying, "I'm going to try to get as close to twenty beans as I can when I take a scoop of these lima beans." Take your handful.

2. Ask the children to help you count the handful. Say that you're going to count by 2s, as a way to count faster. Count out loud with the class.

3. Suppose you scooped up sixteen beans. Ask the children to figure out how far away from twenty you got. Then have volunteers explain how they figured out that you were four away from twenty.

4. Explain that you're going to scoop a second handful, and that you want to hold the sixteen beans in your hand so you'll get a sense for how that many feels. Go on to make a second try, once again counting your total and finding how far away it is from twenty.

5. Explain that the children are now going to have their own chance to try picking up handfuls of twenty. Write the following on the board to guide the children in recording their first and second tries:

Estimating 20

Material: _____

	How Many?	How Far Off?
First Try	_____	_____
Second Try	_____	_____

6. Get the children started on their work by saying something like, "Pay careful attention to what happens on your first try. Use that information to help you get closer to twenty on your second try." (See Figures 3–16 and 3–17.)

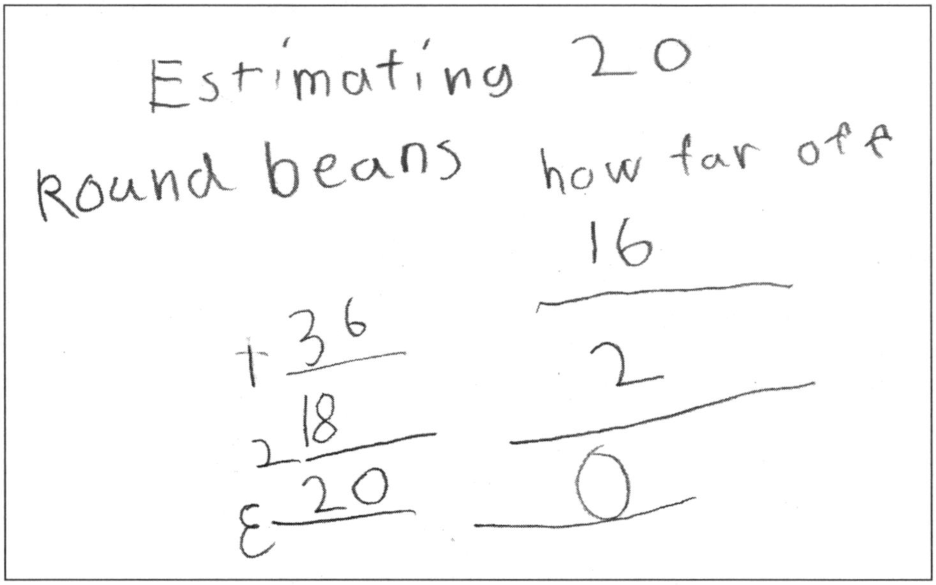

(See Figures 3–16 and 3–17.)

FIGURE 3–16 ▶

Oksana took a large handful on her first try, but came much closer to twenty the second time around.

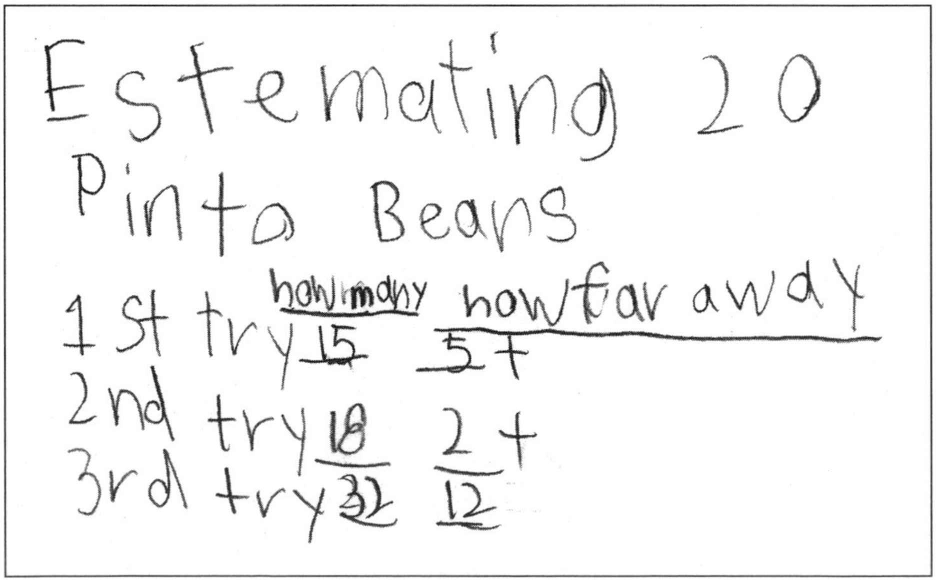

FIGURE 3–17 ▶

Edward improved on his second try, but went overboard on his third try!

Bean-Bag Math

This game comes from *Number Power: Grade 1* (Robertson et al. 1993). Concrete materials that model numeric concepts are important tools for young children. You can make cheap and useful manipulatives that encourage place-value understanding using small plastic bags and lima beans. Players work in pairs.

Materials

- 4 plastic sandwich bags for each pair
- 50 beans for each pair

Instructions

1. Attach a label (adhesive tape works fine) to each bag and label the four bags *5, 10, 15,* and *20.*

2. Have your students put the corresponding number of beans in each bag (see below).

3. Use the bags to form equations. For example, hold up the 5 and the 20 bags and ask a volunteer to tell how many beans there are in all. Write the equation $20 + 5 = 25$ on the board.

4. Hold up three baggies. Talk about the total and how to write the corresponding equation on the board.

5. Encourage students to use their bean bags to write as many different equations as they can by combining any two, three, or four of the bags.

6. Observe your students as they do this activity. Notice which students need to count every bean, one by one through the plastic bags, to determine the total. See which students add larger chunks, mentally saying "Here's ten. If I add five more, that will be fifteen," and so on. Don't interfere with the methods students use to accomplish the task. Remind yourself that they're probably finding the level that works best for them. Those students who are counting one by one need practice doing just that to get a sense of those quantities. Students

who have moved on to more efficient ways of finding the totals are exercising their understanding and giving you valuable information about their thinking.

7. Finish the lesson by bringing the class together and asking volunteers to tell you their equations. Write them on the board, organizing them by their sum. As you listen to each student's equation, ask questions such as:

> "How did you know that fifteen plus five equals twenty?"
>
> "Did anyone make twenty another way?"
>
> "What's the largest (or smallest) number you made?"
>
> "Did anyone get a larger (or smaller) number than that? Why or why not?"
>
> "What numbers were impossible to make?"

Money Trading

Money is inherently interesting to children and can help them understand place value. A single dime represents ten pennies in much the same way that the 1 in 12 represents the quantity 10. With a dime, this idea is easier to understand, because a dime looks different from a penny. But the underlying 1-to-10 relationship is in both the money and the symbolic representation.

The activity sketched below is not presented as a detailed lesson. So before you introduce it, review in your mind all the points you want to make as you teach the game to your students. Pay special attention to the number understandings that might grow out of this game and the questions you might ask students to get them thinking about the possibilities. Think about what you might learn from observing your students do this activity. Consider how you can let them know that you're interested in and respectful of the way they are solving problems.

Materials

- 1 pair of dice per pair of children
- 1 small plastic bag per pair of children
- 30 pennies, 10 nickels, 10 dimes, 1 quarter per bag
- 1 label per bag, to indicate bag contents

Instructions

1. Give students some opportunities to talk about the relative value of pennies, nickels, dimes, and quarters.

2. Announce the game *Race for a Quarter*. The game will help children learn more about the value of these coins and reinforce the notion that *one* of something can represent a group.

3. Gather the dice, and a small plastic bag for every pair of children. Put 30 pennies, 10 nickels, 10 dimes, and 1 quarter in each bag. List the coins and their quantities on a label, then stick the label to bag. That way your students can inventory the contents at clean-up time— and get still more counting practice.

4. Partners take turns rolling the dice, finding the sum, and getting out coins that have the same value as the sum. A child who rolls a total of seven has the choice of getting out seven pennies, or one nickel and two pennies. The winner is the first player to have enough coins to trade for a quarter.

Notes: When you're introducing the game, discuss these different possibilities, but let the children know that they get to decide which coins to use as long as their partner agrees that the coins match the dice total. A player can to decide when to trade coins as long as it is his or her turn. This is a competitive game, so you might want to go over the thoughts about winning and losing discussed in September when you introduced number games.

When the children become proficient with *Race for a Quarter*, they can move on to *Race for a Dollar*. The same rules apply, but this time the goal is to get to a dollar.

Solving Double-Digit Word Problems

Solving word problems enables children to apply what they learned when they played games and did activities aimed at developing number understandings. Although their place-value understandings are probably fragile and incomplete, most second graders can begin to apply what they know about counting to real-world problems. At this time of the year, a few children may also apply what they have learned about grouping numbers to come up with more efficient solutions to word problems. The important thing to remember is that children develop the *ability* to understand and solve word problems by having the *opportunity* to do so.

Children develop their *own* procedures for solving double-digit addition and subtraction problems if given the chance to do so. Over time, their performance of these procedures becomes increasingly efficient. Their methods may even be mathematically superior to the standard carrying-and-borrowing algorithm currently taught in the United States.

Strategies for Solving Double-Digit Word Problems

Before you begin introducing word problems to your students, reflect on some possible solutions to this problem:

You and the teacher down the hall decide to make a second-grade quilt. Each of you has twenty-nine students in your class. How many blocks will the quilt have if each child contributes one block?

Ask yourself:

- What did you do to solve this problem?
- Did you write down the numbers in a column and use the standard carrying method?
- Did you calculate that $29 + 29$ is close to $30 + 30 = 60$, except that you have to subtract 2 (because 30 is one more than 29 and you did that twice), so your answer is 58?
- Did you figure $20 + 20 = 40$ and $9 + 9 = 18$. Now you need to add 40 to 18, so you'll have 58 blocks?
- Did you use some other numeric method that quickly yielded a correct answer?

At this time of year, some second graders may come up with several of these numeric methods—all of which are efficient ways to solve the problem. Some children may even be familiar with the standard U.S. algorithms for adding and subtracting larger numbers. If they can explain the procedures they've been taught, understanding that they are not "carrying a one" but instead moving ten to the 10s place, then they may be able to use this method to solve problems with larger numbers. But know that your role is *not* to teach these rote procedures for solving problems. Why? Most students do not yet have a grasp of place value firm enough to comprehend the mathematics underlying the procedure.

Typically, fall second graders create a model that enables them to count out the answer. Some will make a physical model by setting out cubes to represent both groups of twenty-nine and then count the cubes one by one. Others will use drawings or check marks to keep track of the two quantities. Students who are developing confidence in their ability to mentally visualize the problem may represent only the second group of twenty-nine quilt blocks with cubes or pictures. Their thinking will go something like this: "Our class will make twenty-nine blocks, now I need to count twenty-nine more. So: Thirty, thirty-one, thirty-two . . . " and on up to 58.

These students are each finding their own ways to make sense of the problem. In so doing, they are showing where their mathematical thinking is now *and* they are building their number understandings. Constructing models reveals the structure of the problem; counting builds a sense for larger numbers. The goal for all children is that they eventually become adept at designing efficient numeric solutions. Making sense out of problems is an important step toward meeting that goal.

You and your students will engage in a process that allows:

- *you* to assess your students' current understanding of number and place value.
- your *students* to explore and build their own mathematical understandings about place value.

Your job is to:

- provide problems to solve and make sure students have a chance to visualize and understand them.
- create an atmosphere where children feel comfortable and eager to explore their thinking.
- ask questions that encourage students to reflect on their thinking.
- give students an opportunity to clarify their thinking by talking and writing about their solutions.
- focus your energy on appreciating the many ways students solve problems. You'll gain a deeper understanding of how your children think mathematically.
- assess your students in a relaxed, nonjudgmental way. You'll remind yourself that partial understanding is OK for now, because students will have many opportunities, over time, to strengthen their understanding.

Introducing Double-Digit-Addition Word Problems

Don't go to elaborate lengths when devising word problems for students to solve. An occasional problem that grows out of a piece of literature or involves trips to the grocery store to buy bags of peanuts or candies can add spark to your math program. But on most days, much simpler arrangements should prevail.

For example, prepare a simple problem that involves adding ten pennies to sixteen pennies. The money context of this story isn't particularly important—you could easily use a story that incorporates something you're studying in the class (zoo animals or tide-pool life, for example). The important thing is that the numbers make sense in that context. Choose a context that is familiar and appealing to your students, and numbers that have a sum of less than fifty and require regrouping.

1. Write out the problem on a large piece of paper or on the chalkboard— but cover up the written problem until later.

2. Gather your students in a circle and explain that you're going to tell a story that involves combining groups. Suggest that your students close their eyes and try to visualize the action of the story as you tell it. Emphasize that you'll be asking them to recall what happened in the story, not tell the answer to the combination problem. This kind of introduction encourages the children to focus on the concept of addition and to organize the particulars of the problem in their minds.

3. Tell the story like this:

One day I was counting all the pennies I had collected in a jar. There were sixteen pennies. Later that day, I found ten more pennies in my coin purse. I put those pennies in the jar, too. How many pennies did I have in the jar then?

4. Ask: "Who can retell the story? Remember, I want to hear your version of the story, not the answer to the problem." Have two or three children retell the story. You're likely to get only minor variations of the story, and that's fine. Retelling firmly roots the story in the children's minds. It draws them into the story and into the mathematic relationships expressed by the words. It also creates a quiet, thoughtful atmosphere in the classroom as the children listen to one another.

5. Explain that each person will take a blank sheet of paper and show how he or she goes about solving the problem. Make a statement emphasizing your interest in their *thinking*. Say something like, "I want you to show how you got your answer, because I'm very interested in your thinking. In fact, your thinking is just as important to me as your answer."

6. Explain the mechanics of completing the assignment: "After you write your name and date on your paper, copy this heading onto your paper." Refer to the chalkboard, where you've written an appropriate heading. Say: "Then use words, pictures, numbers, or other symbols to solve the problem." Write these possibilities on the board as you suggest them to the children. Point out: "You may want to use cubes or other materials to help you keep track of the problem. If you do, make sure that you draw or write about what you used."

   The chalk board will look like this:

Pennies Problem

   Solve the problem using:

   words

   pictures

numbers

other symbols

It's fine to use cubes or other counters to help you solve the problem. Tell what you did first, then what you did next, and so on.

7. To illuminate what you mean by "using pictures" or "using cubes," and to give students a starting place, ask for volunteers to tell how they're planning to solve the problem. If your students don't have any ideas, say something like, "What pictures could you draw to solve this problem?" and "How could you use cubes to help solve this problem?" The amount of nudging you'll need to do will depend on how much experience your students have had solving problems. Probe just enough to get the ideas flowing—without coming up with a prescription for solving the problem.

8. Uncover the written problem to make it available for reference.

9. As the children begin working, step back and observe the whole room to see who might need your help first. Go to those tables first. If too many students are unfocused, give reminders to the whole class about working thoughtfully and doing business-talk only. Then circulate among the students to encourage discussion about the problem and keep them focused on their work.

   With students who are having trouble getting started, you may need to say, "What will you do first to solve the problem?" This simple query, and your nearby presence, may give them the focus they need to engage with the problem. Stay a few moments to make sure they've got a starting place.

   With students who are involved in the problem, spend some time just noting how they are going about their work. If it doesn't seem intrusive, ask such questions as, "What do these pictures represent? How did you decide how many circles to draw?"—anything that shows you're interested in their thinking.

10. As children feel that they are finished, they can bring their work to you. If they haven't been clear about how they solved the problem (and at this stage many of them won't be), explain that you need to know more. Say something like, "What did you do first? Then what did you do? Now go back and find a way to show that on your paper. Remember: it's OK to draw a picture of what you did with the cubes. Words and numbers can help, too." Your students may grumble at being asked to write more, but insist that their work be complete in the sense that you can tell *how* they solved the problem. As they get more practice with this process, their work will improve and explanations will become second nature to them.

    Early finishers can play a game that they've learned to play previously.

Sharing Strategies

Many books suggest having a follow-up discussion about problem-solving strategies during the last fifteen minutes of the math period. This may work for you, or you may prefer to wait until the beginning of the next day, when everyone is fresh. The purpose of this discussion is to give students the opportunity to consolidate their understanding by talking about their strategies, and to create a forum in which children can see other ways of solving the same problem. Because you circulated among the children as they were solving the problem and also discussed many of the children's solution as they finished, you'll have a pretty good idea of what your students will be ready to share.

When you ask for volunteers, start with someone who has a solution that involves drawing out and counting all the pennies, one by one. Try to duplicate on the board what the child did on his or her paper. If Sharon says, "Well, first I drew sixteen pennies for the ones in the jar," quickly draw sixteen circles. When she goes on to say, "I drew ten more for the ones in the coin purse," make a separate group of ten circles. If she explains, "Then I counted them all," have the class count with you, writing the numbers in order above the circles, as the class counts up to twenty-six pennies (see below).

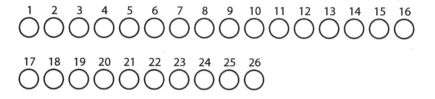

If someone has a counting-on solution, call on that person next. As Marvin explains that he started with sixteen in his head, and then drew ten more circles (or used his fingers to keep track of ten), try to capture his solution on the board as well. Your drawing might look like this:

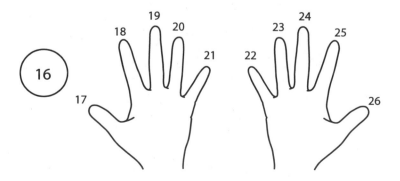

Finally, record any solutions that involve decomposing the 16 and adding a group of 10. For example, Clarissa might talk you through this solution: "Sixteen equals ten plus six. Ten plus ten equals twenty. Then I thought twenty plus six is twenty-six." (See below.)

$$16 \qquad + \qquad 10$$

$$\diagup \diagdown$$

$$10 \quad\;\; 6$$

$$10 + 10 = 20$$

$$20 + 6 = 26$$

It's hard not to be overly enthusiastic when a child comes up with this kind of solution. Try not to value one method over another; instead, respect all the children's efforts equally. Over time, more and more youngsters will be able to use these more efficient solutions. But until they are mathematically mature enough to reason this way, they are only going to feel confused and put down if their methods are devalued. Remind yourself that children become much more persistent if their hard work is seen as valid.

During this solution-sharing session, some children may find it difficult to sit quietly as others explain their solutions. Remind them that being fair and friendly includes listening to and learning from one another. After each solution is presented, ask if anyone else did something similar, to bring more children into the conversation. But keep the pace moving so the session doesn't become overly long.

Introducing a Double-Digit Subtraction Problem

On another day, you'll want to come up with a problem that involves subtraction (separating a quantity into two parts). Something like:

I had twenty-six cents and then I went to the store and bought some penny candy. I spent twelve cents. How much money do I have left?

Go through the same procedure of asking the children to visualize the problem and share their versions of it before sending them to their desks to devise their own strategies for solving this problem. The class's strategy-sharing session will probably yield ideas such as these:

"I used twenty-six cubes for the twenty-six pennies. I took twelve of them away. When I counted, I had fourteen left." (See below.)

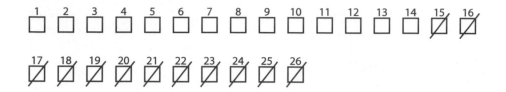

"I counted backwards. I started with twenty-six, and then I went twenty-five, twenty-four, twenty-three . . . . I made sure I counted back twelve, because I put a number above the backward-counting numbers." (See below.)

"Twenty-six minus ten is sixteen, and then sixteen minus two is fourteen [26 − 10 = 16; 16 − 2 = 14]. It's like before I know that twelve is really ten and two. I took the ten away first, because it was easy to do."

Other children may surprise you with a counting-up method that goes something like this: "I started with twelve and then counted up to twenty-six. I kept track with my fingers." (See below.)

12	13,	14,	15,	16,	17,	18,	19,	20,	21,	22,	23,
	1	2	3	4	5	6	7	8	9	10	11

24,	25,	26,
12	13	14

Subtraction and addition are inverse operations, and some children feel more comfortable using addition to find the difference between two quantities. I often apply this method myself when thinking about the difference between two quantities. I leave out the finger counting, but find a way to reason my way through the space between the two numbers.

A Story Problem Menu

To give your students more practice with story problems, make up at least ten more that involve addition and subtraction. Set these out in a menu format so that the kids can solve them at their own rate. Don't expect every child to solve every problem. Use simple situations (children playing on the playground or standing in line for lunch, or animals at the park or zoo). Consider including characters or objects that relate to a current topic of study in your class. Use numbers in the 20s, 30s, or even higher for those who are ready for them. But adjust downward for a child who needs more work with small numbers.

To add variety to the menu, use a few of the games mentioned earlier that the children are already familiar with. Also, make time to discuss certain problems with your students. Warn your students a day or two beforehand that "on Tuesday we'll be sharing strategies for Problem 3 on the menu. Make sure you've solved that one so you'll be ready to talk about it on Tuesday." Children who finish all of the problems can write problems of their own. You can then duplicate these for others to solve.

Number Puzzles

This activity helps children get to know the orderly sequence of numbers on a 1–100 chart. Students practice this skill by making a puzzle for the class and, later, by using puzzles made by fellow students.

Materials

- blank 10-by-10 Grid for Number Puzzles (see page 82 and Blackline Masters), preferably run off on heavy stock paper, 1 for each child
- envelopes large enough to hold the puzzle pieces, 1 for each child

Instructions

- Day 1: Each child fills in the numbers 1–100 on one of the blank grids. After the grid is filled in, the children the margins off and discard them, then cut the grid into seven pieces. Encourage them to make cuts on the lines, and to use shapes other than rectangles. The child writes his or her initials on the back of each of the seven pieces. Before depositing the pieces in an envelope, he or she tests to see that the pieces fit back together again, and writes his or her name in a prominent place on the envelope.
- Day 2 and in the future: Students try out each other's puzzles, fitting the pieces together using the shape and number clues. After successfully putting together a puzzle, a child may add his or her name to the back of the envelope.

1	2	3	4	5	6	7	8	9	10
11	12	13	14	15	16	17	18	19	20
21	22	23	24	25	26	27	28	29	30
31	32	33	34	35	36	37	38	39	40
41	42	43	44	45	46	47	48	49	50
51	52	53	54	55	56	57	58	59	60
61	62	63	64	65	66	67	68	69	70
71	72	73	74	75	76	77	78	79	80
81	82	83	84	85	86	87	88	89	90
91	92	93	94	95	96	97	98	99	100

Assessing Place-Value Understandings

You may not have time to formally assess every child's place-value skills, but I strongly recommend finding time to interview at least three children. (See Wickett and Burns 2002.) Choose one child who you think has strong number skills, one average student, and another child who is struggling. You will learn an enormous amount about how fall second graders think about our number system by asking these students questions in a gentle, nonjudgmental way. If you have time to assess every child, you'll gather invaluable information for talking with parents about their child's progress. (See Figure 3–18, Figure 3–19, and Figure 3–20.)

Here is a recommended approach to assessment:

Part 1: Grouping by 10s

1. Give the child a set of twenty-four cubes and ask her to group them by 10s.

2. Ask: "How many groups of ten do you have, and how many ones are there?" "How many cubes is that in all?" "Please write the total."

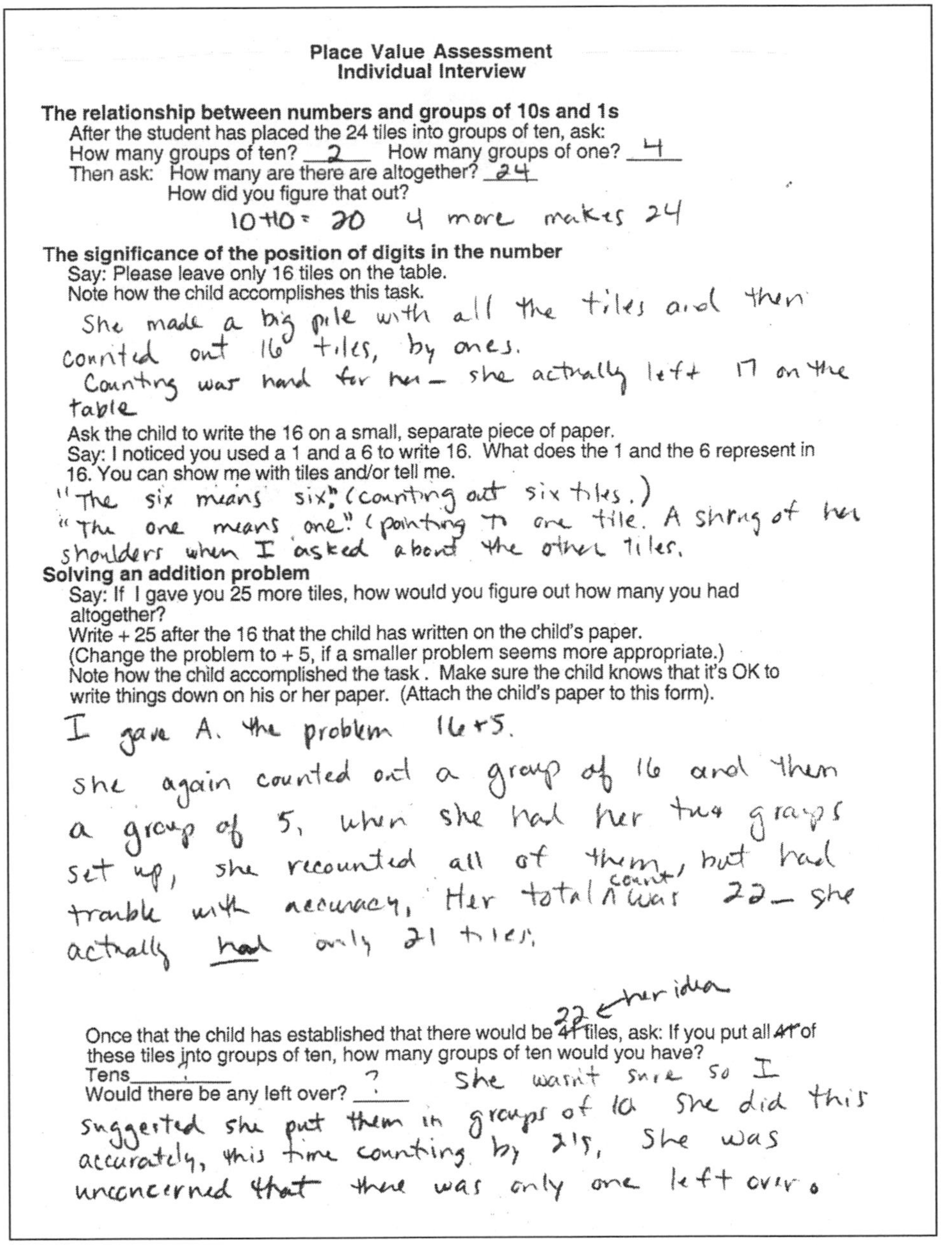

FIGURE 3–18 ◀

Place Value Assessment
Individual Interview

The relationship between numbers and groups of 10s and 1s
After the student has placed the 24 tiles into groups of ten, ask:
How many groups of ten? __2__   How many groups of one? __4__
Then ask: How many are there are altogether? __24__
How did you figure that out?

10+10= 20   4 more makes 24

The significance of the position of digits in the number
Say: Please leave only 16 tiles on the table.
Note how the child accomplishes this task.

She made a big pile with all the tiles and then counted out 16 tiles, by ones.
Counting was hard for her — she actually left 17 on the table

Ask the child to write the 16 on a small, separate piece of paper.
Say: I noticed you used a 1 and a 6 to write 16. What does the 1 and the 6 represent in 16. You can show me with tiles and/or tell me.

"The six means six" (counting out six tiles.)
"The one means one" (pointing to one tile. A shrug of her shoulders when I asked about the other tiles.

Solving an addition problem
Say: If I gave you 25 more tiles, how would you figure out how many you had altogether?
Write + 25 after the 16 that the child has written on the child's paper.
(Change the problem to + 5, if a smaller problem seems more appropriate.)
Note how the child accomplished the task . Make sure the child knows that it's OK to write things down on his or her paper. (Attach the child's paper to this form).

I gave A. the problem 16+5.

she again counted out a group of 16 and then
a group of 5, when she had her two groups
set up, she recounted all of them, but had
trouble with accuracy. Her total count was 22 — she
actually had only 21 tiles.

22 ← her idea

Once that the child has established that there would be 41 tiles, ask: If you put all 41 of
these tiles into groups of ten, how many groups of ten would you have?
Tens_____   She wasn't sure so I
Would there be any left over? __?__
suggested she put them in groups of 10   she did this
accurately, this time counting by 2's. She was
unconcerned that there was only one left over.

Most second graders can do the grouping by 10s and many can figure out the total using the groups. Watch for how confident the child is, and whether she needs to count from 1.

Part 2: Thinking About What Digits Represent

1. Say: "Now you need only sixteen cubes. Please leave sixteen cubes on the table." Note whether the child needs to count, starting at 1, all the way to 16, before removing the eight extra cubes. A more

Figure 3-18 caption:
Alicia didn't understand the position of the digits in a large number and had problems counting large numbers accurately, but she did understand that 16 + 5 means to combine the two quantities. She needed to count all the tiles to get an answer.

FIGURE 3–19   ▶

Ricky seemed to understand the 1 in 16 represents a group of 10. He counted accurately and was able to count on, rather than counting all the tiles.

Place Value Assessment
Individual Interview

The relationship between numbers and groups of 10s and 1s
After the student has placed the 24 tiles into groups of ten, ask:
How many groups of ten? __2__   How many groups of one? __4__
Then ask: How many are there are altogether? __24__
            How did you figure that out?

10 and 10 are 20 and then 21, 22, 23, 24

The significance of the position of digits in the number
Say: Please leave only 16 tiles on the table.
Note how the child accomplishes this task.

He took 2 handfuls - counted them and figured out he had 12 tiles so far. He used his fingers to count up to 16 (13,14, 15,16). And then knew he needed to get 4 more to make 16.

Ask the child to write the 16 on a small, separate piece of paper.
Say: I noticed you used a 1 and a 6 to write 16. What does the 1 and the 6 represent in 16. You can show me with tiles and/or tell me.

the 1 means a ten (He made a group of 10)
the 6 means six (pointed to the six extras)

Solving an addition problem
Say: If I gave you 25 more tiles, how would you figure out how many you had altogether?
Write + 25 after the 16 that the child has written on the child's paper.
(Change the problem to + 5, if a smaller problem seems more appropriate.)
Note how the child accomplished the task. Make sure the child knows that it's OK to write things down on his or her paper. (Attach the child's paper to this form).

He tried counting with his fingers from 16. He got confused. So, he decided to get out 25 more cubes - counted accurately.
He then said, "This 16" - pointed to original 16.
He then used the 25 new cubes to count on "17, 18, 19... → 41."

Once that the child has established that there would be 41 tiles, ask: If you put all 41 of these tiles into groups of ten, how many groups of ten would you have?
Tens___4___
Would there be any left over? __1__

confident child may take one group of ten and count out six more to create a group of sixteen—or use some other method that shows she has a well-developed sense of quantity.

2. Ask the child to write the number *16*. Say: "Can you tell me what the one in sixteen represents and what the six represents?" Frequently, fall second graders will not know that the 1 in 16 actually represents a group of 10. They will state that the 6 represents six 1s and that the 1 represents one. Other students may have a firm—or fragile—understanding that the 1 actually represents a group of ten.

FIGURE 3–20 ◄

Angel understood that the 1 in 16 represents a group of 10; her decision to count up from the larger number suggested that she should be encouraged to think of yet another way to solve 16 + 25.

Place Value Assessment
Individual Interview

The relationship between numbers and groups of 10s and 1s
After the student has placed the 24 tiles into groups of ten, ask:
How many groups of ten? __2__ How many groups of one? __4__
Then ask: How many are there altogether? __24__
How did you figure that out?

She said, "10, 20, 24."

The significance of the position of digits in the number
Say: Please leave only 16 tiles on the table.
Note how the child accomplishes this task.

She took away 4 from one of the tens. Then she took the 4 ones away, leaving a group of ten and 6 ones.

Ask the child to write the 16 on a small, separate piece of paper.
Say: I noticed you used a 1 and a 6 to write 16. What does the 1 and the 6 represent in 16. You can show me with tiles and/or tell me.

the 6 means six
the 1 means a ten   I knew 10+6=16

Solving an addition problem
Say: If I gave you 25 more tiles, how would you figure out how many you had altogether?
Write + 25 after the 16 that the child has written on the child's paper.
(Change the problem to + 5, if a smaller problem seems more appropriate.)
Note how the child accomplished the task. Make sure the child knows that it's OK to write things down on his or her paper. (Attach the child's paper to this form).

Angel first counted, using her fingers to keep track, starting with 25. She said she had started with 25 because "I didn't have to count so much."
I asked her to think of another way to add 25 to 16 and she did the attached work.

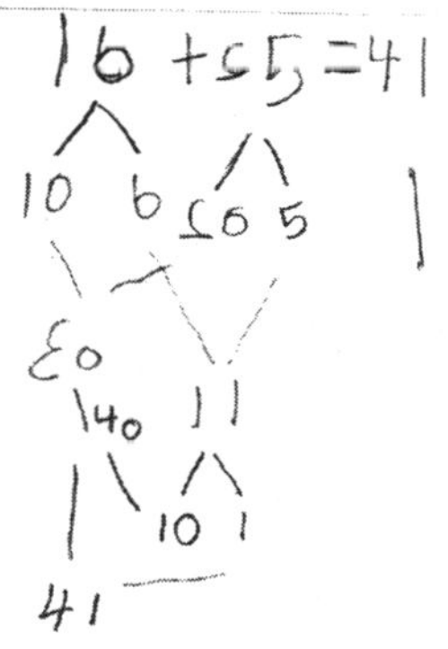

16 + 25 = 41

Once that the child has established that there would be 41 tile
these tiles into groups of ten, how many groups of ten would
Tens __4__
Would there be any left over? __1__

41

Part 3: Solving an Addition Problem

1. Ask: "How would you figure out the number of tiles I would have if I added twenty-five more tiles?" If the child responds that she would get out twenty-five more tiles and count them one by one, you might want to scale the problem back, changing it to adding just five more tiles. Be open to any solution the child comes up with. Your job is to note what the child does. Expect some kids to be able to count on from 16. Still others may solve the problem using groups of ten.

2. Once the child has come up with an answer, have him check his work with cubes. (There should be forty-one if the child added the full twenty-five cubes.)

3. Ask: "If I put these forty-one cubes into groups of tens and ones, how many tens would there be, and how many ones?" Some children will have no way to think about this problem; others may feel confident. By noting all responses, both oral and nonverbal, you'll deepen your understanding about how second graders think about place value.

A Parent Newsletter

You may want to help parents understand something about how their children learn mathematics. The letter in the Blackline Master section of this book can be modified to suit your particular parent community. Some teachers like to send it home with the kids in the fall; others like to wait for the spring, when students are a little further along in their understanding and use of place value. This letter is a slightly modified version of one from my book *Getting Your Math Message Out to Parents*, which may give you other ideas about how to communicate with parents.

Dear Families,

We're now in the middle of a math unit that focuses on developing understanding about our place-value system. This newsletter will give you an in-depth look at how your child is learning to add and subtract.

The way your child is doing mathematics in school likely looks somewhat different from what you remember from your own elementary-school days. Most of us learned to add and subtract using a particular algorithm (a rule or procedure for solving a problem). To add, we were taught to "carry," and to subtract we learned to "borrow." We did pages and pages of computation problems that were unrelated to any particular mathematical context. These assignments were designed primarily to help us remember the steps of the procedure that we had seen in class.

Because these methods are familiar to us, we tend to think of them as a standard for judging computational competency. Unfortunately, students frequently learn these algorithms without connecting them to the meaning of the numbers in a problem. And many adults who learned math this way are unable to figure out simple real-life problems. Algorithms were invented to streamline the process by which we compute. They are useful tools, but because they allow us to bypass understandings about place value, they are a place to end, not the place to begin.

The shortcoming inherent in our standard carrying and borrowing procedures is that they focus attention on the individual digits in the numbers rather than on the quantities that the numbers represent. Students who forget the steps of the procedure find themselves making fairly outlandish errors without even realizing they've made a mistake. And even when they do follow the procedures accurately, they often don't understand why they got a correct answer. Here are some examples of mistakes that students commonly make:

$$
\begin{array}{r}
58 \\
+\ 25 \\
\hline
713
\end{array}
\qquad
\begin{array}{r}
53 \\
-\ 16 \\
\hline
43
\end{array}
\qquad
\begin{array}{r}
{\scriptstyle 4\,9} \\
\cancel{5}\cancel{0} \\
-\ 37 \\
\hline
12
\end{array}
$$

The good news is that there are many efficient ways to solve computation problems. In fact, second graders are very capable of constructing their own procedures. Suppose a problem calls for adding 58 and 25. Second graders often solve this type of problem as follows:

- Add 50 and 20 to get 70.
- Add 8 and 5 to get 13.
- Add 70 and 13 to arrive at the correct answer of 83.

This method is as efficient as the "carrying" algorithm, is easy to keep track of, results in numbers that are easy to work with, and takes seconds to carry out. It is superior to the standard algorithm from a mathematical standpoint, because the problem solver never loses sight of what the digits represent. And it can be generalized to any problem.

Most of us don't know that other cultures have historically used algorithms that are different from those currently taught in U.S. schools. The following examples, from an article by Randolph A. Phillip titled "Multicultural Mathematics and Alternative Algorithms," published in the November 1996 issue of *Teaching Children Mathematics*, shows that some adults from other countries were taught the same procedure in their schools that many of our second graders devise:

An older man educated in Switzerland and a man schooled in Canada in the early 1970s both demonstrated that they had learned to add by starting from the left-most column. The man from Switzerland worked the following two problems:

$$
\begin{array}{r}
59 \\
+\ 16 \\
\hline
60 \\
15 \\
\hline
75
\end{array}
\qquad
\begin{array}{r}
481 \\
+\ 926 \\
\hline
1300 \\
100 \\
7 \\
\hline
1407
\end{array}
$$

This algorithm is one that many elementary-school children in the United States invent when encouraged to do their own thinking. That is, when asked to add multidigit numbers, most children naturally begin adding the digits with the largest place value. This is quite natural for adults as well. For example, if two friends emptied their wallets to pool their money, would they first count the $20 bills or the $1 bills?

Of course, solving the problem with the approach shown above requires knowledge of how a two-digit number is composed of a multiple of 10 and 1s, and how numbers can be taken apart and recombined. Children learn these concepts in class through games, opportunities to build mathematical models using manipulative materials, classroom discussions, and the chance to solve many problems. When faced with the task of adding two double-digit numbers together, the children use what they've learned about our number system to come up with a procedure that they understand in order to arrive at an accurate answer. Students have a profound understanding of an approach that they've constructed themselves, *and* they make many fewer errors by using it.

In the case of both addition and subtraction, it is not possible simply to tell children a procedure for doing a problem. Truly understanding what it means to combine two quantities to get a new quantity is a *mental* relationship that children have to forge themselves. The logical-mathematical knowledge needed to solve both addition and subtraction problems develops over time, arising out of many experiences. We need to respect and encourage children as they move through the natural stages of learning. That process can be uneven and is likely to include periods of confusion as well as learning. Children need a chance to form and reform their thinking as they develop understanding.

Students typically go through several stages when learning to add and subtract. For example, some might solve the problem above by starting at 58 and counting on 25 ones (59, 60, 61, 62, . . . 83). These students have developed an understanding of the meaning of 58 + 25. If carried out accurately, this method will give a correct solution. However, counting by 1s becomes unmanageable and is prone to errors as numbers get larger. Our goal is to help children find more efficient methods of adding and subtracting. Over time, they will learn to chunk numbers in an addition or subtraction problem so that the numbers are easier to work with. We find that students frequently develop efficiency in solving addition problems before they develop efficiency with subtraction.

The procedures that students develop in the primary grades can be applied to larger problems. When faced with a problem like 1462 + 1745 + 278, students have no need for the old carrying algorithm. Instead, they might approach the problem like this:

- 1000 + 1000 = 2000 and 400 + 700 + 200 = 1300. That brings the total so far to 3300. (Jot that figure down to keep track of it.)
- Next calculate 60 + 40 + 70 = 170. Now the total is up to 3470. (Jot that number down.)

- Now it's a simple matter of adding $2 + 5 + 8 = 15$ to bring the total up to 3485.

Note that it hasn't even been particularly important to line the numbers up vertically. The child has jotted down only three figures to keep track along the way. And most important, the problem solver can feel confident about the answer because he or she has remained focused on the quantities represented by the numbers, not the individual digits. Approaches like this one are efficient and accurate for solving virtually any problem we might reasonably encounter in life. You might want to try making up some hypothetical problems yourself to get a feel for how this approach works.

In the past, too many children ended up disliking mathematics and believing—wrongly—that they were not good at it. We need to turn that perception around. Mathematics is all about making sense, so we need to teach it in such a way that the sense-making is always apparent. If young children have the opportunity to build a firm foundation of *understanding* in the realm of number, they discover that they can achieve mastery over an important part of our world.

Warmly,
Nancy

Chapter 4

December

CATEGORICAL DATA COLLECTION

The Learning Environment

The month of December is short, with the weeks between the Thanksgiving and winter breaks often interrupted by other schoolwide events. You might find yourself saying, "I'm going to use this month to finish up the number work we began earlier in the fall. My students are really starting to make sense of our number system, and I want them to have a little more time with the concepts I've introduced." Or you may be saying to yourself, "I sense a certain restlessness in the children. I know they have more to learn about number this year, but we'll come back to it in the early spring and we need a change of pace. I need to find something that matches the growing exuberance of the season. Data collection just might work for us now." ∎

Choices are never easy, and I'm convinced that the reason I go home so tired from teaching every night is that I have to make so many decisions each day. But there's no easy way around this dilemma if we want to present a mathematics program that is truly tailored to our students' needs. When making these decisions, remember that there is no perfect second-grade curriculum for all children. Trust yourself to make good decisions based on what you observe your students doing every day.

Even if you plan to focus primarily on the number work begun earlier in the fall, take a few minutes to skim the data-collection ideas suggested below. You might find ways to incorporate some of these activities into other classroom subjects such as science or social studies, now or later in the year.

Today's Number and Calendar Making

Continue the daily routine of *Today's Number*. Make sure you have plenty of "unrestricted" days—that is, days with no particular rule imposed—so the children can explore their own numeric ideas. But don't hesitate to impose a rule when you feel that it will help focus students' attention on a concept the class is studying. For example, as part of your warm-up on day 64, you might say something like: "What do you know about the number sixty-four?" You'll be looking for such comments as:

- It's an even number.
- It's a multiple of 2.
- It has six 10s and four 1s.

Model some of the above statements if your students don't come up with them. Go on to pose questions such as "Is sixty-four closer to sixty or closer to seventy? Is it closer to fifty or closer to one hundred?" When asking these kinds of questions, have a large 1–100 chart available. Before you send the children to their tables to make equations, ask, "What are some equations for sixty-four that start with fifty? What about some equations that start with one hundred?"

If you haven't done so already, you might want to begin using a class list that allows you to check off children's names each time they share an equation. Don't forget to give fair warning to those children who need to share in upcoming days. Also, set aside a period when your students can make a December calendar, noting the special days of the season.

The Mathematics

The need to interpret data accurately looms large in today's data-infused world. You can help your students feel comfortable in this arena by modeling ways to gather, represent, and interpret data and by giving students opportunities to do these same tasks independently. The activities listed below often involve children talking to each other—but also encourage them to stay on task. The work often also entails drawing. Thus minds *and* hands are kept directed and busy.

Teacher-Organized Data Collection

Graph Types and Topics

Young children are especially interested in data about themselves. So begin by creating some simple charts on which students record personal information. For example, you could ask students to choose their favorite season, or you might make a line plot to document something about eye color in your class. (See Figure 4–1.)

When you create a graphic display for students to fill in, you're modeling one of many ways to collect and display data. For instance, you could include pictographs. (See Figure 4–2.)

Consider bar graphs as well. (See Figure 4–3.)

Choosing Topics

Choosing subjects for graphs requires sensitivity on your part. A graph about the holidays that each family celebrates in December may be a way

FIGURE 4–1 ▶

Students placed an X on the graph to show if their eyes are brown, blue, green, or hazel.

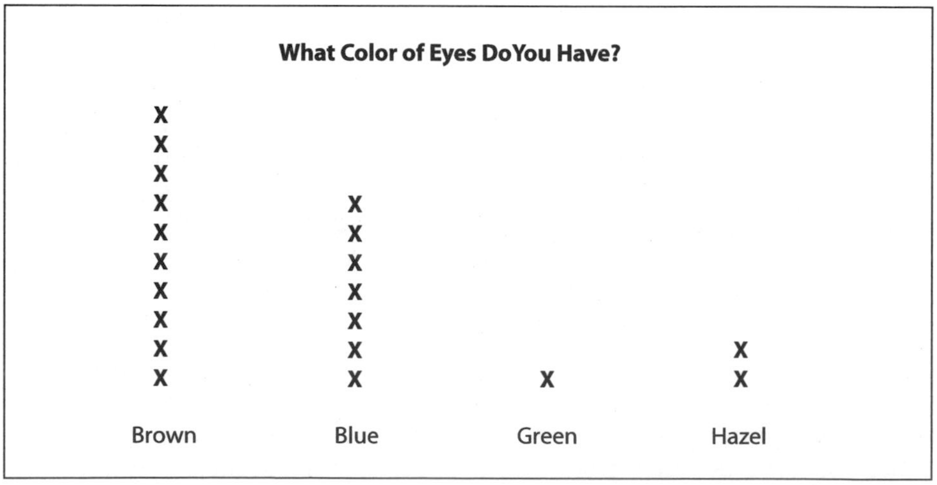

What Color of Eyes Do You Have?

| Brown | Blue | Green | Hazel |

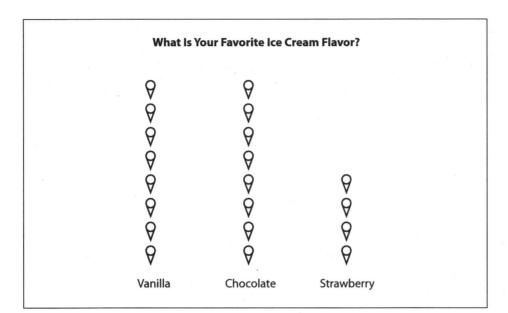

FIGURE 4–2   ◄

Students used pictures of ice cream cones to show their favorite flavor.

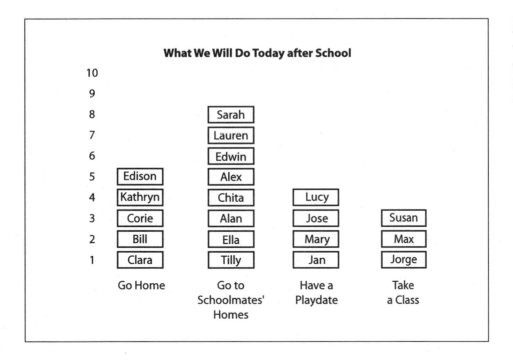

FIGURE 4–3   ◄

This bar graph is made from placing students' names in different categories.

of celebrating diversity in one classroom. In another, this same topic may make a child feel excluded. So make sure you think through these issues before you choose a topic for a graph. Generally, children love to share information about themselves and their favorite foods, colors, pets, etc.

Data Collection from Home

You can connect home and school by asking students to collect data at home, as a homework assignment. This exercise will help parents understand what you are doing in the classroom. It also gives children a chance to collect data on a wide variety of neutral topics, such as birthplace, favorite foods, types of pets, favorite pastimes, etc.

Assembling a Graph in the Classroom

Once you've chosen a topic and given the children a chance to gather their data, think through how you'll have each child add his or her information to the graph. If you decide to make adding data to the graph a class experience, find ways to help the children stay focused while they are waiting their turns. Proximity to the graph itself can help some children stay engaged, so consider putting the graph on the floor and gathering the children around it. Make the process of adding data fast and snappy, with occasional stops to ask focusing questions such as:

> "What do you notice so far?"
>
> "How many more brown-eyed people than blue-eyed people do we have so far?"
>
> "Now that we've got data from half of the class on the graph, what do you think the most popular ice-cream flavor will be?"

If students have trouble staying focused on the process, especially once their own data has been added, or if you have a large number of students, try an alternative way to assemble the graph. Begin by having a class lesson during which the students discuss the topic of the graph. This discussion gives children a chance to think about their individual choices and lets them know what form their data will take on the graph (an X, a picture, a cube, etc.). You can then assemble the graph later, during an activity time (when children are playing other math games, for instance) by asking a few children at a time to add their data to the graph.

Analyzing a Class Graph

When is the best time to analyze the data in a graph; that is, take time to notice things about it? You might best do this a few days after all the data has been posted and the graph has been displayed in a prominent place where the children can see it as they go about other activities. Giving the children a chance to get to know the graph through casual observation helps them become familiar with the data. You may also want to set a class goal of noticing at least ten things about the data, over the course of the next few days. Explain to the children that today you will call on five volunteers to describe what they notice about the graph. Tomorrow, five more people will have a chance to offer their suggestions. Dividing up the discussion this way keeps it from becoming tedious. It also creates anticipation among the children, as they think about coming up with ideas. If your students are engaging in this type of observation/discussion for the first time, help them focus by asking question such as:

> "Who can tell us something about how the number of people with brown eyes compares with the number of people with blue eyes?"
>
> "Is there anything about this graph that surprises you?"
>
> "How many people posted their favorite type of ice cream on this graph?"

These nudges help the children know what kinds of observations are appropriate when analyzing data.

Student-Created Projects

Eventually, you will want to give students opportunities to take more responsibility for all aspects of data collection. Deciding what data to collect—and then collecting, representing, and analyzing a body of data—encourages responsibility among students. Children who select their own categories for organizing data must think flexibly as they encounter the overlapping categories that inevitably arise from real-world data. Help them by introducing group activities that encourage students to think flexibly about how to categorize data and reexamine their ideas as they analyze more information.

Getting Started: People Sorting

Data collection almost always involves sorting and categorizing information, because graphs are designed to present information quantified in easy-to-discern displays. So part of helping children develop data collection skills should include activities that provide opportunities to notice and sort the attributes of a set.

People-sorting games, such as the one described in *Mathematics Their Way* (Baratta-Lorton 1994), are valuable ways to start. People sorting involves grouping children based on some obvious physical attribute, such as who is wearing shoes with laces or wearing shirts with long sleeves. Based on your students' past experience with sorting activities, decide how explicit to be about which attribute you're using to sort the class. The first few times, you may need to be very explicit by saying something like, "Today we're going to sort ourselves by the types of shirts we are wearing. Those of us who are wearing shirts with buttons will come up to the front of the room. Let's look at Kayla. Does she fit my rule? Yes, she has buttons, so she should come up. Raise your hand if you think you should be standing next to Kayla." After you've added a few students to the button group, seek out some examples of people who do *not* have buttons on their shirts. Ask those students to stand in another area. You don't need to sort the whole class—just enough so the children understand the rule you are using.

At other times, when you sense that most of the children understand the concept of sorting by an attribute, you'll want the class to be able to guess your (unstated) rule for sorting the class, based on careful observation. When you feel that students are ready for this level of reasoning, explain that you're going to play a game that will require them to "read your mind." Be sure to choose an easily visible attribute, such as whether someone is wearing a sweatshirt.

Explain that the class has the job of figuring out your "mystery rule" based on where you ask students to stand. Make this a silent game, explaining that you want everyone to have lots of time to think, so no one should tell an idea until you ask them to. After you've motioned several students who fit your rule to move to the front of the room, invite silent volunteers to point to someone else who might fit the rule.

Make it clear that you'll be the final judge of who joins the group at the front of the room: "If a person is chosen who does not fit my rule, we might be able to get valuable information by looking at that person. So we'll make a separate place for people who do not fit the rule." Once again, impose the rule of silence until several volunteers have made their suggestions.

When you feel that many children have discerned your rule, let students take turns saying what the rule might be. Encourage them to explain their reasoning, and ask questions such as:

"Did anyone have an idea about the rule when we first started that changed as more people were added to the group?"

"What made you sure of the rule?"

Each time you play this game, record the number of students who do and don't fit your rule. Use this opportunity to show that there are a variety of ways to record data. For example, you might use numbers one time. Another time, tally marks in groups of five. Another time, use simple pictures that relate to the topic in some way. (See Figure 4–4.)

Once the children understand the game, you can let volunteers take over your role. Brainstorm possible topics as a group or individually to make sure students understand that the attribute determining the rule needs to be easy to see. (People who have dogs as pets, for example, would not be a good mystery rule for this game.)

Self-Portraits and Data Collection

Now you'll want students to begin doing their own data-collection projects. One approach that may work involves having children collect data

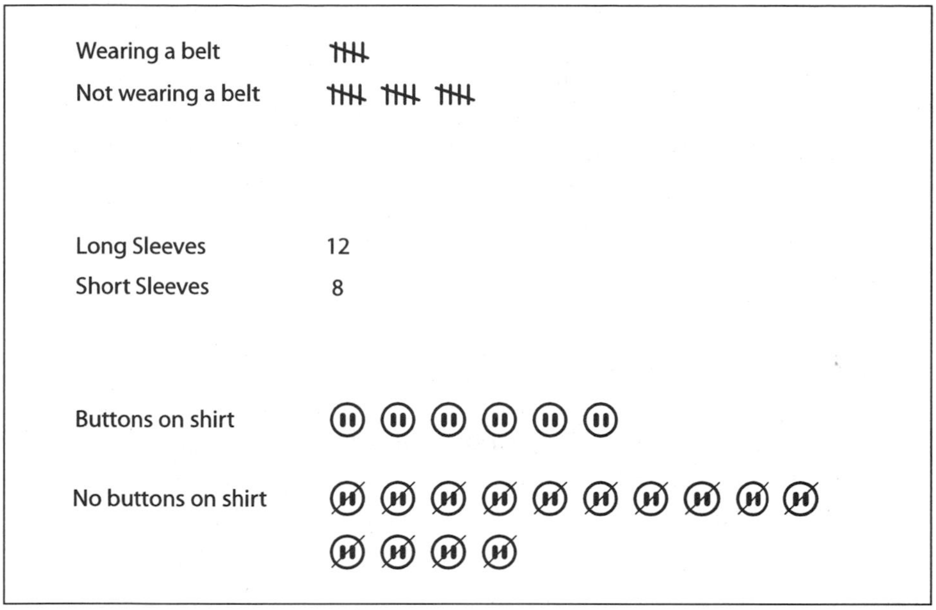

Wearing a belt   ⊞⊞

Not wearing a belt   ⊞⊞   ⊞⊞   ⊞⊞

Long Sleeves   12

Short Sleeves   8

Buttons on shirt   ⓘ ⓘ ⓘ ⓘ ⓘ ⓘ

No buttons on shirt   Ⓜ Ⓜ Ⓜ Ⓜ Ⓜ Ⓜ Ⓜ Ⓜ Ⓜ Ⓜ Ⓜ Ⓜ Ⓜ Ⓜ

FIGURE 4–4 ◀

Three examples of tally marks that students can use to collect data.

that they observe in a class set of drawings. Have your students each make a new self-portrait. Let them know beforehand that this time you'll be displaying the portraits around the room for others to observe carefully. To prepare for this activity, have on hand one or two existing portraits or self-portraits done by artists. Ask the children to describe what they notice about one of them. Use the questions below, or those of your own devising, if students need help getting started:

"What colors do you notice?"

"What interesting shapes or lines did the artist use?"

"Do you think this portrait was made long ago or just recently? Why?"

"What does the portrait tell you about the person in the picture?"

Before the children draw their own self-portraits encourage them to show not only what they look like, but to also add details, like holding a ball, that show their interests. When all the portraits are completed, post them around the room, at a level that lets observers notice details about each. Get permission from a few students to use their work for another round of careful observation. In that round, ask some of the same questions you used for the art prints. Finish this discussion by pointing out some attribute of one of the portraits:

"I wonder how many people in our class used the color red."

"I wonder how many people put a ball in their self-portraits."

"I wonder how many people pictured themselves inside a room."

Explain that each person should do these tasks:

- Make a short list of things to wonder about in regards to the self-portraits.
- Select one of those things to gather data on (by observing all of the portraits and noticing how many of the portraits had the chosen attribute).
- Decide how to keep track of how many portraits have the chosen attribute.

Then set a time for students to do the following:

- Observe each of the self-portraits and gather the data.
- Tell the story of the data, by representing it in a pictorial way on a piece of plain paper. Remind students that they can use tally marks, pictures, numbers, or any other form of representation to show how many of the self-portraits had the attribute and how many did not.

FIGURE 4–5 ▶

Edison noticed how many self-portraits had black shoes.

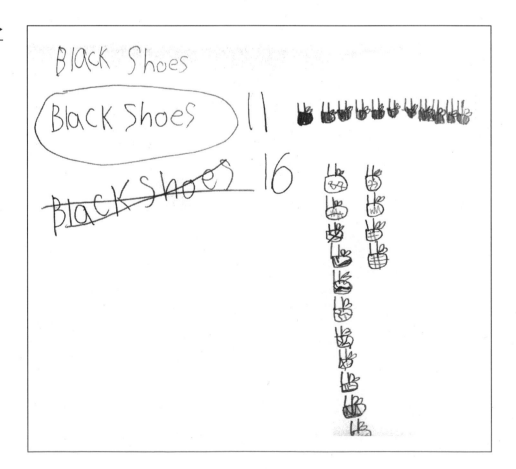

FIGURE 4–6 ◄

Jan was Edison's partner. She collected the same data but represented it in her own way.

After a brief discussion about what it means to work thoughtfully during such an assignment, give students time to examine all the self-portraits and collect data about their chosen attribute. As children finish, they should return to their seats and begin representing the data. (See Figures 4–5, 4–6, and 4–7.) Circulate from table to table, asking questions such as these to encourage them to do thoughtful work:

"Have you made sure to indicate what attribute you were looking at?"

"Is it easy for someone looking at your work to tell how many people did and did not include your chosen attribute?"

FIGURE 4–7 ◄

Alex used tally marks to show how many people drew themselves wearing gray.

"Have you found a way to make you work eyecatching, so a viewer is interested in your work?"

Don't be surprised if their first attempts leave out many of these details. But don't hesitate to gently prod them, with your questions, to make their work more complete.

When the data-collection period is over, decide whether you want students to present their findings to the class. If you do, give them time to practice what they plan to say. Break the presentation up into time segments that match students' attention span.

Collecting Data Through Interviews

Students can also choose a topic, gather data, and represent the data by conducting interviews with one another. This time they won't need to confine themselves to observable attributes, because they'll be able to talk to one another. To use this method, they first need to devise a question that prompts interviewees to choose one of two interesting ideas. They then interview each classmate, find a way to record each person's answer, and

FIGURE 4–8 ▶

Carlos interviewed his classmates during a science unit on tide pool life. He asked, "Would you rather be a hermit crab or a mussel?"

finally represent the data in an interesting way. Eventually, you may want to ask students to present their findings to the class.

Possible topics could include:

"Would you rather be very famous or live forever?"

"Would you prefer to study marine mammals or forest inhabitants in science?"

"Do you like to buy your lunch or bring it from home?"

You might schedule this activity as follows:

- Day 1: Introduce the project and let students develop their questions.
- Day 2: Students interview one another. Set ground rules for doing this process in a purposeful manner.
- Day 3: Give students time to tell the story of the data by representing it with words and pictures.
- Day 4: Have students share their findings with the class. Keep listening periods to a reasonable length of time. Have more than one session if necessary. (See Figure 4–8.)

Working with "Messy" Data

In real life, data is often messy. Categories overlap, and it is not always clear-cut how to organize the data. To illustrate this point, ask students to write down a favorite food on a 3-by-5-inch card. Give them a chance to illustrate their own personal food choice, then gather the cards in a pile. With the class seated in a circle, go through the cards, deciding which ones should go together. The class may initially think that ice cream should go in the same category as milk, since they're both dairy products—until a card with apple pie comes along. Maybe the pie and ice cream should go together, because they're both desserts, and the milk belongs in a separate category with other drinks. This activity gives you a chance to talk about the importance of reexamining data to form new categories as more data comes along. It also enables you to point out that there isn't one "right" way to organize the data.

After this discussion, have pairs of students organize and represent another body of data that the class has collected. This data could be about the children themselves or be related to a science topic that the class is studying. For example, suppose you suggest the topic *What Was Your Favorite Thanksgiving Break Activity?* Give each child a large sticky note on which he or she can write a few words and draw a simple picture to show a favorite activity. Or if you are studying animal habitats, you might ask each child to write a brief description of one animal's habitat. In this case, the children could provide this information on a large sticky note with a simple drawing.

FIGURE 4–9 ▲

Data from nine different children about their Thanksgiving break artwork.

Once you've collected data from each child on the chosen topic, arrange the sticky notes on pieces of legal-sized paper and duplicate enough copies so that every pair of students has a complete set of the data. (See Figure 4–9.)

Your students can now cut their duplicated set of the data into separate pieces and then decide, together with their partners, how to sort the information. For this stage of the activity, provide paperclips so the children can keep their sorting choices organized into groups. Also provide an envelope for them to store their bits of paper at the end of the session.

The next task is to decide how to represent this data. You might ask each child to do his or her own representation, or invite partners to work together to create one representation. Figures 4–10 and 4–11 examples of student work.

Students find it helpful to have some models to get started. So don't hesitate to sketch some possible ideas to show them, or make an overhead of the student examples presented here. Remind the children that their work should be eyecatching and clear.

Once the children have completed their representations, encourage them to think about what they would like to tell the class about their work before

FIGURE 4–10 ◀

Ella and Alan created eleven different categories and represented their data with checkmarks to show the quantities for each category.

you have a class sharing session. The sharing session gives everyone an opportunity to see the many different ways that the same set of data can be organized and represented by different people.

FIGURE 4–11 ▶

FIGURE 4–11 ▶

Kelly came up with eight categories using the same data. Her representation makes it clear whose data she placed in each category and includes numbers as well as symbols.

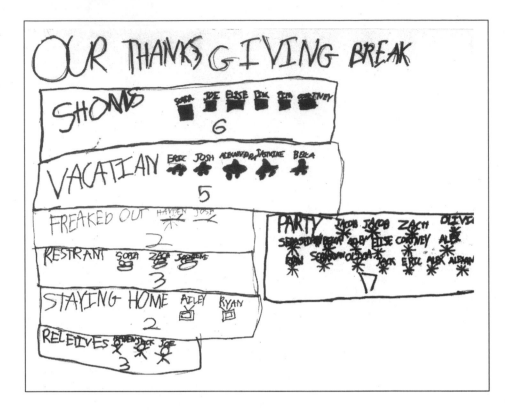

Venn Diagrams

If you played name-sorting games in September, your students will have some familiarity with Venn diagrams. Consider using such diagrams now in a literary situation. One possibility is to read several of the *Frog and Toad* books by Arnold Lobel, emphasizing observations about each of the two main characters. When your students know these characters well, work together to fill in a two-circle Venn diagram with *Frog* as the label for one circle and *Toad* as the label for the second.

Ask students to notice how the two characters are different from one another. For every statement about Frog, try to come up with an example for Toad that describes a way in which Toad behaves differently than Frog. For example, if someone says Frog is adventuresome, ask what you might write about Toad. Someone will probably notice that Toad prefers to stay in bed. After you have several examples of the characters' differences, fill in the intersection with ideas that are true of both of them. Figure 4–12 shows a finished diagram.

You might also use a Venn diagram to compare two versions of the same folktale. Or use a Venn to think about a scientific topic your class is studying, such as habitat. One example might involve placing animals in these categories: those that live on land, and those that live in the water—with an intersection for animals such as seals, amphibious animals, or insects that live in either habitat during different life stages.

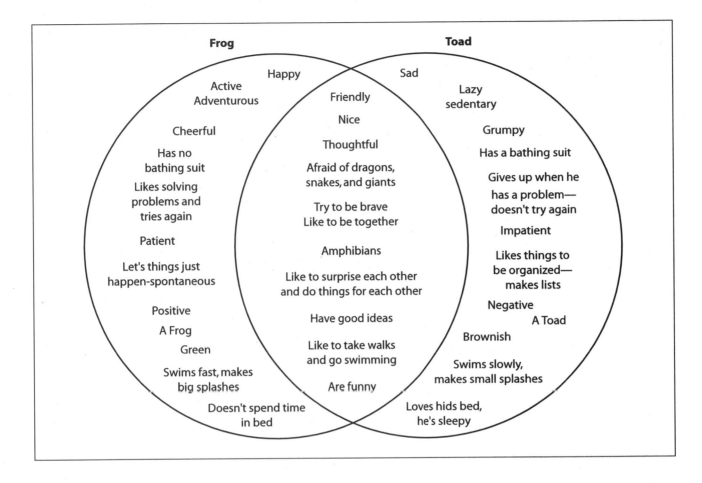

Frog

Happy

Active
Adventurous

Cheerful

Has no
bathing suit

Likes solving
problems and
tries again

Patient

Let's things just
happen-spontaneous

Positive

A Frog

Green

Swims fast, makes
big splashes

Doesn't spend time
in bed

Friendly

Nice

Thoughtful

Afraid of dragons,
snakes, and giants

Try to be brave
Like to be together

Amphibians

Like to surprise each other
and do things for each other

Have good ideas

Like to take walks
and go swimming

Are funny

Toad

Sad

Lazy
sedentary

Grumpy

Has a bathing suit

Gives up when he
has a problem—
doesn't try again

Impatient

Likes things to
be organized—
makes lists

Negative

A Toad

Brownish

Swims slowly,
makes small splashes

Loves hids bed,
he's sleepy

Data Collection

My favorite data-collection activity for second graders involves having them experiment with a group of small items, noting which of them sink and which float. (See Figure 4–13, Figure 4–14, and Figure 4–15 on the following pages.) This project and many others involving categorical data can be found in *Does It Walk, Crawl, or Swim?* (Russell et al. 1997).

FIGURE 4–12 ▲

**Frog and Toad Venn
diagram.**

FIGURE 4–13   ▶

Bill created four sink/flat categories.

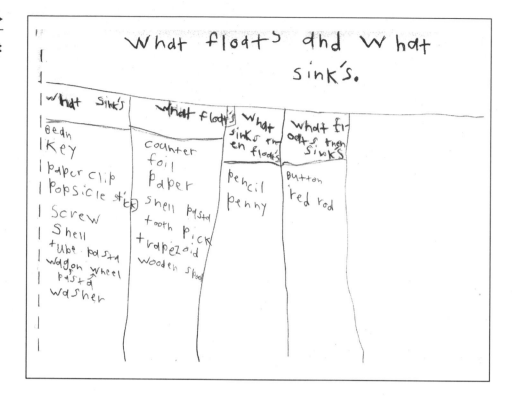

FIGURE 4–14   ▶

Clara used a Venn diagram to show her results.

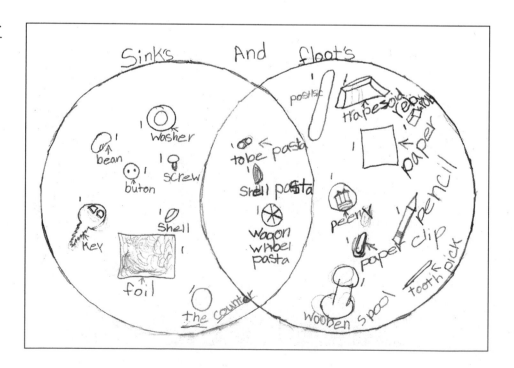

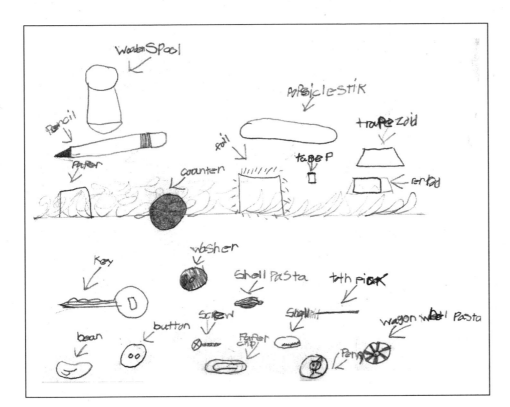

FIGURE 4–15   ◄

Tilly drew a picture of the items in the tub of water and carefully labeled each item.

Chapter 5

January

GEOMETRY

It's time to turn to geometry and the world of space. Much of what people do in real-world mathematics has to do with space. Professionals in the construction trade constantly apply number understandings to shapes and angles. So does a homeowner when calculating the amount of wallpaper needed to spruce up the bathroom. And so does a grandparent when thinking about the design of a quilt for a new grandchild.

Geometry can open a door into the world of mathematics for some children. Indeed, a child who is not particularly adept with number may show great understanding of shape. Geometry activities provide opportunities for these children, in particular, to thrive. ■

The Learning Environment

Children come to school having had many everyday experiences with shapes. They've played with toys in the form of geometric shapes and watched an adult cut an apple in half so it can be shared with a friend. In the classroom, you can build on these experiences—linking school mathematics to space and form in fun and exciting ways.

In teaching geometry, your job is to help students:

- become increasingly familiar with the language of geometry through activities that ask them to identify and classify shapes by their attributes.
- develop strong visual and spatial skills through activities revealing that geometric shapes can be broken down or composed of other shapes.

Geometry for primary-school students has been less rigidly defined than work with number—even in today's standards-driven world. So you may feel freer to experiment with what works best for you and your students. You can learn how to balance class lessons with independent (menu) activities and base your pedagogical choices on how your students are responding.

Some of the lessons below are described in detail to serve as models. Others are more briefly described, so you can decide how to introduce the activity to your students. The chapter ends with a list of resources that you may want to turn to for additional ideas.

Today's Number and Calendar Making

During this period, when you are focusing most of your attention on shape, doing *Today's Number* (see Chapter 2) can be a great way to keep number alive in your classroom. If you haven't already been using this routine, this could be a good time of year to begin. Use the calendar date as the target number for the equation total each day.

Most of the time, you will want students to write equations without imposing rules on them. But don't hesitate to make suggestions on some days. For example, if you want to ensure they are reviewing their combinations for 10, make that your rule of the day. (For instance, $9 + 1 + 8 + 2 + 5 + 5 + 4 = 34$.) This may be a good time to require equations that are composed of multiples of 5 ($15 + 20 + 10 + 5 - 15 = 35$). Or have an all-doubles day ($10 + 10 + 5 + 5 + 3 + 3 = 36$). Whenever possible, show the relationship between one equation and the next. For example, that last equation could be decomposed further to become $5 + 5 + 5 + 5 + 5 + 5 + 3 + 3 = 36$. That way, your students continue to think about number relationships.

The children will probably also be eager to make a calendar to start out the new year. Set aside a period when they can complete this monthly ritual.

The Mathematics

You may want to start with an introductory exploration, such as *The Four-Triangle Problem.* This activity requires little in the way of materials except for shapes cut from construction paper, scissors, and glue. It introduces students to some geometry vocabulary *and* provides many opportunities for spatial problem solving.

The Four-Triangle Problem

Day 1

Materials

- 3-by-3-inch construction-paper squares, in two contrasting colors, at least five or six of each color per child
- newsprint or old newspaper cut into 9-by-12-inch rectangles, five or six per child
- small, clear bags
- scissors for each child
- glue
- 1 large sheet of paper labeled *Geometry Words,* and a pen (or the chalkboard)
- 7 18-by-24-inch sheets of plain newsprint
- 7 sentence-strip labels marked as follows: *Triangles, Squares, Rectangles, Parallelograms, Trapezoids, Pentagons, Hexagons*
- a place on the rug for the shapes to be sorted
- a place on the wall to display the shapes in an organized way

Instructions

Use these steps as a warm-up:

1. Put bags of the 3-by-3-inch squares and sheets of the 9-by-12-inch newsprint at each table.

2. Explain that today the class is going to be exploring geometry, the mathematical study of shapes.

3. Hold up one of the 3-by-3-inch squares and ask if anyone knows the name of this shape. Spend some time discussing the properties of a square by asking volunteers to describe the shape. Your students may comment on the color of the square, the number of sides it has, the fact that all four sides are the same length, and the number of corners.

4. On the *Geometry Words* list, record the words *square, sides, corners,* and any other words that come up that seem appropriate. You may want to add the word *angle* and explain that it's a mathematical term used to describe a corner.

5. Model how you can fold one square, corner to corner, to create a diagonal fold. Open the square, use the term *diagonal* to describe the fold, then cut along it. Ask if anyone knows what new shapes you've made. Spend some time discussing the properties of the triangles you've made. Record the words *diagonal* and *triangle* on the *Geometry Words* list.

6. Tell the students to take one of their own squares, fold it diagonally, and cut along the fold to make two triangles. Ask them to see if they can put their two triangles together to form the square again.

7. Now pose a new problem: "I want you to see how many different shapes you can make using your two triangles. There's one rule you must follow: When you put your triangles together, the sides must touch all the way from one end to the other, and the sides that touch must be the same length." You may want to show some examples of arrangements that fit the rule and some that do not. (See below.)

This arrangement
fits the rule

These do not

8. Say: "When you've made a new arrangement that fits the rule, glue it onto a piece of newsprint." Model how to apply glue to the edge of each triangle to glue it to the newsprint.

9. Say: "After you glue your first new shape together, fold and cut another square on the diagonal to see if you can make another new shape. See how many different shapes you can make following the rules of this activity."

10. Circulate among the children as they work, encouraging them to keep searching for new shapes. When everyone has glued down at least one shape, ask for everyone's attention.

11. Ask a volunteer to bring one shape up to be posted. (The two new shapes that can be made are a triangle and a parallelogram.) Children can indicate with a show of hands if they made the same shape. Take the time to name the new shapes, adding the word *parallelogram* to the *Geometry Words* list after everyone has had a chance to say the word aloud.

Now introduce the larger exploration, which will take up the rest of this math period and at least one more whole period. In the coming weeks, this exploration can be used as an independent activity for as long as your students are interested in it.

Instructions

1. Say: "We've been making new shapes with two triangles. Now we're going to see what shapes we can make with *four* triangles. You and your partner will each take one square, fold it, and cut it on the diagonal. If your partner takes a red square, you should take a yellow one. Together, you'll see what new shape you can make by putting all four of your triangles together. You must still follow that rule about the sides having to be the same length and touching completely." Demonstrate by putting together and gluing down a four-triangle shape yourself. (See below.)

2. Say: "This time, when you've made a new shape using four triangles, glue it on the newsprint. Then trim around the shape so all the

extra newsprint is cut away." Demonstrate this step by cutting around your four-triangle shape.

3. To create interest in the project, ask, "Who has a prediction about how many new shapes we can make if we follow the rules using four triangles?" You may want to take a moment to go over expectations by encouraging volunteers to reiterate the rules and procedures of the activity in their own words. Try to avoid questions posed in a testing format ("What do we call this shape?"). Instead, phrase your questions in ways that encourage reflection. For example:

   "Who has a way of describing the rule about sides touching that you have to follow when making your new shapes?"

   "What else do you need to keep in mind in order to work thoughtfully on this task?"

   "Can you remember what we call the fold that goes corner to corner on the square?"

   "Can anyone remember the name of this shape?" (Point to the parallelogram.)

4. Circulate among your students as they make their own four-triangle shapes. As you go from table to table, further the children's geometry vocabulary by asking them to count the number of sides on the shapes they've created. Make comments such as, "Ah, you've made a shape with five sides. We call all five-sided shapes pentagons."

   Some children will need help counting the sides of their new shapes. They may especially get confused by shapes that have a long side that is half one color and half another color. Demonstrate how to count the sides by running your finger along each side as you count it. Once a shape is cut out, you can flip it over. Your student will then be able to see the sides without the distracting color changes.

5. End this first session by asking the children to clean up and to leave their shapes to dry on their tables—or in another spot you've designated.

Day 2

On Day 2, children will explore ways to sort the shapes they've made.

Instructions

1. Before you gather on the rug, have the large newsprint sheets and sentence-strip labels of the shape names nearby. Make sure there's room to spread out all the pieces of newsprint.

2. Ask the children to join you in a circle on the rug with their shapes. Partners should sit next to each other and place their shapes on the

floor in front of them. Say: "Make sure your hands are not on your shapes, so everyone can see all the different shapes you've made. Today we're going to sort the shapes. Does anyone see any shapes that might go together? Let's think about the number of sides each shape has."

3. Place the suggested shapes on one of the large pieces of newsprint. You may end up with three triangles, only two of which have the same color arrangement. Discuss how the shapes are the same, but note the different color arrangements. Place the *Triangles* label on the newsprint with the shapes, keeping only the shapes that are not duplicate color arrangements. (See below.)

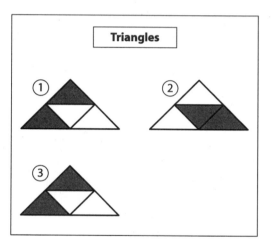

Shapes ① and ② have different color arrangements.

Shape ③ is a duplicate of shape ① and should not be posted.

4. Work together to sort the rest of the shapes by placing them on pieces of newsprint with the appropriate labels. Here's where the art of teaching comes in. It's better to have a short, focused discussion that introduces the idea of sorting the shapes by their number of sides than to sort every shape. So try to pull students into the discussion by introducing the interesting idea that any shape that has six sides is called a hexagon. But stop before interest flags in the sorting process. Any shapes that are not placed on the appropriate spot can be added by their makers once the class has gone back to making more shapes.

5. Explain that for the rest of the period, partners will work together gluing new four-triangle shapes. Say: "When you've glued one new shape together on a piece of newsprint, trim away all the extra newsprint. Then bring your shape down to the rug and place it where it belongs." Continue to circulate, chatting with children as they create new shapes and place them on the appropriate piece of newsprint.

Menu Possibilities for **The Four-Triangle Problem**

Below are strategies for maintaining students' interest in *The Four-Triangle Problem*.

Adding New Shapes

At the end of the day, transfer the shapes to the wall, organized by shape with the corresponding label. On subsequent days, students who produce additional shapes can check to see if they've come up with a new arrangement or if they have duplicated one that is already displayed.

One way to encourage interest in finding new shapes and arrangements is to say something like, "Look at the trapezoids. I see a trapezoid that has a yellow square in the middle and blue triangles on each side." (See below.)

Ask, "Does that arrangement give you an idea for a new arrangement?" If no one offers the suggestion of a trapezoid with a blue square flanked by yellow triangles, point out two other shapes that are negatives of each other. (See below.)

Helping children see possibilities encourages them to persevere and introduces the idea that their work can be focused rather than random.

Four-Patch Quilt Designs

Children take great pleasure in designing quilt blocks, an activity that provides a real-world example of how people use geometry. In this activity, students will arrange eight half-square triangles in two colors to form a larger square. (See below.)

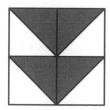

This activity serves as an extension of *The Four-Triangle Problem,* as students discover that they must follow the rule about same sides touching that they encountered when putting their four triangles together.

Each child eventually has an opportunity to choose a favorite design and then replicate it several times. These blocks are then glued down to form a pleasing whole. Putting the blocks together to form a larger unit allows students to explore the way orientation affects the resulting overall design of their quilt. (See below.)

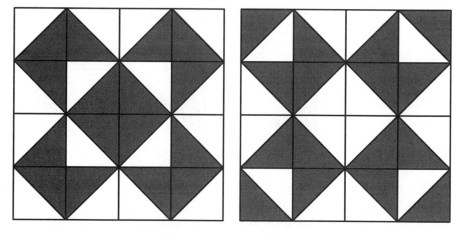

The same four blocks take on a different look
when they are oriented differently.

Making a Quilt Block

Materials

- half-square triangles in a variety of colors, based on a 4-by-4-inch square (see below)

- 8-by-8-inch squares made of construction paper or newsprint, to serve as a backing for the blocks—use 2 or 3 per student for the free exploration phase and 16 for each completed quilt
- glue
- 1 pocket chart or other vertical space to display the blocks
- 32-by-32-inch squares to serve as a backing for the completed quilts

Instructions

1. Gather students in a circle on the rug. Place a variety of colors of triangles on the space in front of you, along with one 8-by-8-inch backing square.

2. After a brief discussion about your plan to make a paper quilt, model the notion of making a personal decision about which two colors to use. Pick up one triangle and hold it next to several of the other colors, commenting on which combinations appeal to you.

3. Once you've decided on your two colors, explain that you'll need eight triangles—half of them green (for example) and half of them purple. Ask: "How many of each color will I need to make my quilt block?"

4. Count out the four triangles of each color and then begin placing them onto the 8-by-8-inch square. Explain that you want to cover the large square completely, with nothing sticking over the sides. Use the time during which you are moving your triangles around to explain how to do the activity and to model the notion of looking carefully and reflectively at design possibilities. Quickly put together one arrangement and then say, "Hmm, that's interesting, but I wonder what other arrangements I can make." (See below.)

This arrangement lets me see lots of triangles.

5. Move a few triangles around to see how these changes affect the design. Spend a moment or two noting the new shapes that form as you move triangles around.

6. Settle on a design to glue down. (See below.)

Now I see a trapezoid and fewer triangles.

As you're gluing, ask the students if they think the rule from *The Four-Triangle Problem* about same-length sides touching applies to this activity. Don't push for a definitive answer; instead, encourage children to think about this idea as they make their own blocks.

7. Now that you've modeled how to construct a single quilt block, use this activity as an item on a menu. Or have the whole class begin experimenting with design possibilities. As students work on new designs, remind them about your earlier question about the connection between this activity and the rules governing *The Four-Triangle Problem*. Before moving on to the next stage, students should have a chance to make at least two or three different four-patch designs.

Making a Paper Quilt

Materials

- at least 4 blocks of the same design that follow some sort of color rule—see below for some color rule ideas

- optional: *Eight Hands Round* (Paul 1996), an alphabet book of quilt designs. Each quilt design is pictured both as a single block and as a quilt made up of several blocks of the same design. If you have access to this book, share it with your students sometime before you introduce quilt-making activities.

Instructions

Once your students have had a chance to make several quilt blocks of different designs, it's time for them to choose one, replicate it several times, and then put all the blocks together to form a "quilt." This step bridges the gap between mathematics and art, doing double duty in terms of curricular areas. You may want to schedule this work during your art time.

Getting started on a quilt involves lots of decision-making:

■ *You* need to decide if you want students to work alone or in pairs. A completed quilt takes at least nine blocks, but having twelve or sixteen to work with is even better. Second graders can generally handle this much work alone, but it does take time. Working with a partner can be fun, but may require making compromises. And you also have to deal with the issue of who takes home the completed quilt.

■ Your *students* will have to choose which four-patch design they want to base their quilts on.

Children will also need to make a color rule to follow. Examples of color rulcs include:

■ Use the same two colors on all the blocks.

■ Keep one color constant in all the blocks, but vary the second color of each block. (See below.)

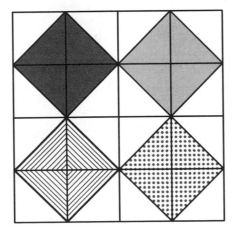

■ Use the same two colors throughout the quilt but in the opposite places in half the blocks. (See below.)

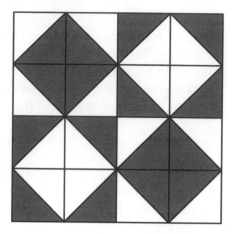

■ Make half the blocks in one color combination and the other half of the blocks a different, but complementary color combination. (See below.)

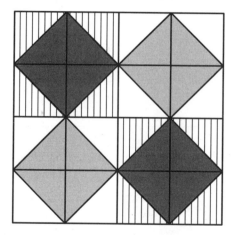

■ Make every block different.

Have some examples of these color rules when you demonstrate putting quilt blocks together.

Of course, children will also ultimately have to decide how to arrange the completed blocks to form a whole.

Use these steps to conduct the activity:

1. To introduce the idea of creating a larger quilt, put your four quilt blocks together to form a square. Talk about how you decided on a particular color rule for your blocks, but mention at least one other

possible rule. Then try to elicit additional color-rule possibilities from your students.

2. Show how changing the orientation of the blocks in relation to one another affects the overall pattern of shapes. Explain that once they've made four blocks of their favorite design, the kids can begin playing around with different possibilities. But mention that they should make their final decisions about how to place their blocks after they have all sixteen blocks completed.

3. Encourage students to make decisions about how to proceed. Now the job of making paper quilts can begin!

4. As the kids work, invite them to explore with color tiles how many blocks they need in order to create a quilt that is either square or rectangular.

5. Once the students have completed all of the blocks they plan to include in their quilt, encourage them to try many possible arrangements before they glue down their blocks on the large piece of backing paper.

Tangram Activities

The books *The Tangram Magician* by Lisa Campbell Ernst and *Grandfather Tang's Story* by Ann Tompert can serve as delightful introductions to tangrams, ancient Chinese puzzles created by cutting a square into seven specific shapes. Read one of these stories in class as a way to get students interested in cutting their own shapes and doing activities with shapes.

Cutting Tangrams

Materials

- 6-by-6-inch squares of construction paper, 1 per student
- scissors for each student
- 1 envelope for each student, to store the tangram pieces after they are cut

Instructions

The sketch below shows how to cut the seven tangram pieces from the square. Have your students follow you, step by step, so they will each end up with their own tangram set. They should store their pieces in an envelope to use in the following activities. You may find that students need more than one set of tangrams to do all the activities you plan for them. You can go through the step-by-step process of cutting them again, or you can encourage the children to figure out for themselves how to cut a second set.

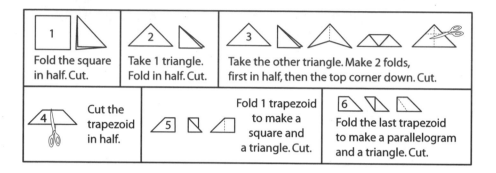

Tangram Puzzles

Materials

- 1 set of tangram pieces cut by each student
- pieces of $8\frac{1}{2}$-by-11-inch paper

FIGURE 5–1 ▶

Rocket shape puzzles

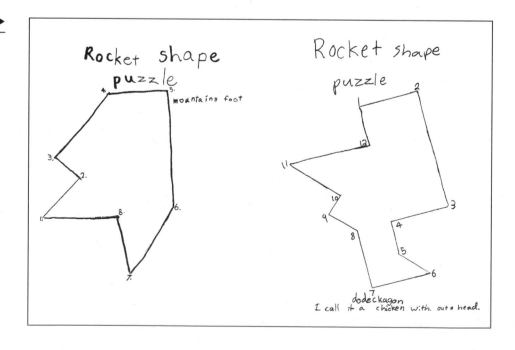

Instructions

Students form a picture using all seven of the tangram pieces. They then trace around the outline of their picture. They label it with both a mathematical and personal name. (See Figure 5–1.) These "puzzles" are then available to other students who try to fit their tangram pieces into the outline.

Side-by-Side Tangrams

Materials

- 1 set of tangram pieces for each student—commercial or hand cut from paper

Instructions

Student 1 makes a design using a complete set of tangrams. Student 2 copies the design using his or her tangram pieces. While Student 2 looks away, Student 1 moves a piece of the design; Student 2 then tries to figure out how the design has changed. Partners should first do this activity sitting side by side and then sitting across from one another. Ask, "Which way is easier? Which way is harder?"

This simple activity is great for providing opportunities for spatial problem solving. Partners can take turns creating and copying the designs. Try this yourself with a partner to see how the spatial problem solving changes when you shift from side by side to across from each other.

A Tangram Graph and Class Book

If you've read one of the tangram picture books mentioned above, you may want to have your students make a class book based on one of them. Each student can contribute one tangram "transformation" to the book. Before putting the individual pictures together to form a book, help students sort their tangram pictures, display their work as a graph, and finally add text to the pictures to create a book that flows from transformation to transformation.

Materials

- $8\frac{1}{2}$-by-11-inch watercolor paper or plain construction paper and watercolors
- 1 set of tangram pieces cut by each student
- glue

Instructions

1. Make the background first; have your students swirl watercolors on a piece of white watercolor paper, or opt for something simpler by

using construction paper in a color that contrasts with the tangram pieces.

2. Next, students cut a new set of tangram pieces from construction paper. (Use the instructions on page 122.)

3. When the background is dry, encourage the students to try out many different arrangements of their tangram pieces before deciding on a final "transformation" to glue down. You can make the rule that no one may glue any pieces down until a certain amount of time has passed by, in order to encourage thoughtful work (ten minutes, at least).

4. When all the individual tangram pictures have dried (probably on another day), put them in a pile and have your students join you on the rug.

5. Choose two pictures that have something in common and place them in the center of the circle. (For example, both of the pictures might depict a creature that flies.)

6. Explain that the class will be sorting the pictures by attributes. These attributes will be determined by the class as you go along.

7. Ask if these two pictures should go in the same group or in separate groups. Encourage two or three students to give their opinions and explanations for their reasoning. Break ties by taking a quick vote.

FIGURE 5–2 ▶

A tangram graph that shows different categories.

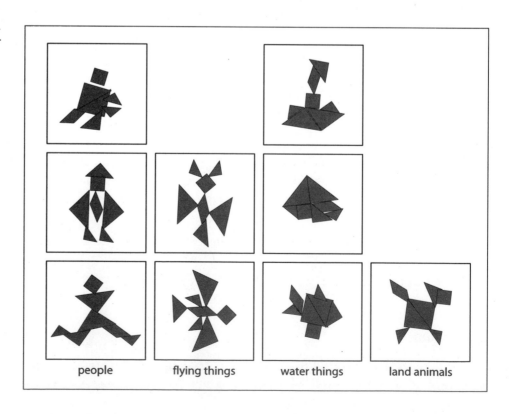

| people | flying things | water things | land animals |

FIGURE 5–3   ◀

Sample from the class tangram book.

He decided to go out and buy a tie and become a very rich man.

When he returned to earth he wanted to have something to eat. So he got a job testing out new dog biscuits. As a dog, he liked them.

8. Now add a third picture, and continue the process of discussing which pictures belong in the same groups. Be open to changing categories as new ideas come up. This kind of discussion can give you new insight into how the children think—and may even reveal a student who is an especially good logical thinker.

9. When all the work is sorted, display the picture on the wall in labeled rows, creating a sort of graph. (See Figure 5–2.)

10. After the display has been up for sometime, work with the whole class to decide which picture will come first in your book, which one second, and so on. Have volunteers dictate text, which you then write in the book. Figure 5–3 shows how one group of children began their book.

Pattern-Block Activities

Free Exploration

Second graders automatically create beautiful designs when given a chance to freely explore pattern blocks. You can encourage them to make elaborate, symmetrical designs that explore the relationships among the shapes' angles by having a few designs for them to copy. Start with any block in the center and then radiate out in all directions. Make your design permanent by gluing down paper pattern-block pieces.

Hexagon Fill-In

Using pattern blocks to fill in the outline of a shape provides practice with decomposing and recomposing shapes—a big idea in geometry. It also encourages children to explore the relationships among the pattern blocks. Use the hexagon pattern (see Blackline Masters), or purchase books or activity cards that provide many different shapes to be filled in.

Six Green Triangles

How many different shapes can your students make with six green triangles following the rule that the sides must be touching completely? Children can first create shapes using the pattern blocks and then cut them out of triangle paper duplicated on green ditto paper. Ease them into the activity by having them, as a class, try making shapes with two, then three, then four, then five triangles. They can glue the paper shapes on a piece of paper and label them. (See Figure 5–4.) Then individually, they can try the six triangles.

FIGURE 5–4 ▶

This student shows different shapes made with six triangles.

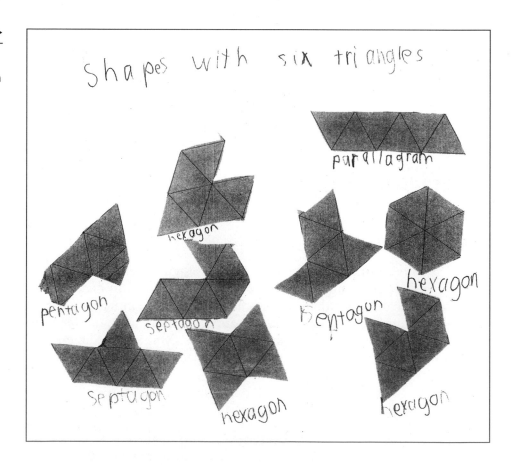

Geoboard Activities

Shading Half a Square

Materials

- 1 geoboard for every 2 students
- rubber bands in containers; 1 container for every 2 students
- geoboard dot paper (4 images on the front of a page—see Blackline Masters); printed back to back, 1 for every 2 students
- geoboard minibooks, made by cutting one sheet of the double-sided dot paper into quarters and then stapling the 4 pieces together

Instructions

1. Gather students on the rug in front of the chalkboard. Draw at least four large circles on the board. Then ask if anyone has an idea of where to draw a line that would divide one of the circles into two halves. A volunteer will likely draw either a vertical or horizontal line that bisects the circle.

2. Shade in one of the resulting semicircles.

3. Tell the class that you want to shade in half of each of the other circles, making each one different. Ask for volunteers.

4. By the time three volunteers have made their marks, you may have the possibilities shown below:

5. Ask if anyone has a new idea, and suggest that it would be OK to draw more than one line. If no one makes the suggestion, show this idea:

6. Now ask: "Could anyone prove that I've really shaded in half of this circle?" Someone is likely to come up with the idea of moving one of the shaded quarters next to the other shaded quarter to make a complete half. Obviously, you can't do this movement on the board. That's good—because it introduces the idea that we can mentally move shapes around to convince ourselves that something is true.

7. Show a geoboard that has a rubber band stretched out so it touches all of the outside nails to form a square. (See below.) Establish the perimeter of the square of nails. Otherwise, the children may think you're talking about the perimeter of the geoboard itself.

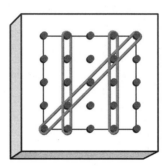

8. Demonstrate how you can now use additional rubber bands to create new ways to divide the geoboard into regions. Explain that when you record an idea on a piece of dot paper, you will shade exactly half of each square. (See below.)

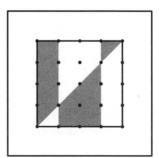

9. Have partners work together, dividing their geoboard along interesting lines and then shading half a square on the geoboard paper.

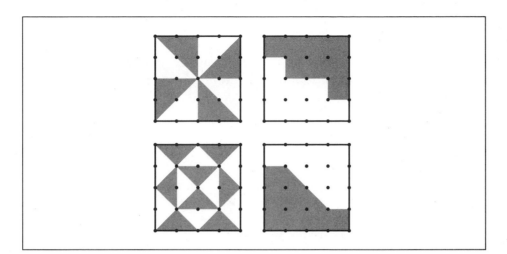

FIGURE 5-5   ◀

Students find ways to divide squares in half and record their results in minibooks.

10. At the end of the period or first thing the next day, have students share some of their favorite ways of shading in half the square. During this group session, ask the children to explain how they can "prove" they have filled in exactly half the square.

Half-Square Minibooks

Each student finds more ways to divide the squares in half. They record their explorations in one of the geoboard minibooks described in the "Materials" section above. (See Figure 5–5.) As you circulate among the children during menu time, ask them how they know that they've shaded in exactly half the square.

Additional Geometry Activities

Math By All Means, Geometry, Grades 1–2 (Confer 1994) provides a complete unit on geometry. Some of my favorites are described below.

Hold and Fold

This activity can help you introduce a unit of geometry. It might be especially useful if your students did *The Four-Triangle Problem* in first grade. It provides opportunities to introduce the names of shapes as your students engage in spatial problem solving.

Rocket Shapes

Students explore how to cut a $4\frac{1}{4}$-by-$4\frac{1}{4}$-inch square into four pieces, which they can then rearrange to form a "rocket shape." (See below.) Once they figure out how to cut the square to achieve the rocket shape, encourage them to rearrange the four pieces to make new puzzles—as with the tangram puzzles described above.

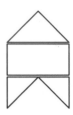

Shapes, Halves, and Symmetry (Cory, Russo, and Akers 1996) describes two of my favorite activities (see below).

Covering Pattern Blocks

Students find all the ways to use other pattern blocks to cover each of the pattern blocks they've already used.

Build the Geoblock

Students are challenged to put other geoblocks together to create a shape the same size and shape as the largest rectangular prism in their current set of geoblocks.

Chapter 6

February/ March

ADDITION AND SUBTRACTION

During February and March, your students will continue to have many opportunities to explore their own ways of solving addition and subtraction problems. They'll be encouraged to communicate with one another about their solutions, and will become less dependent on your guidance during routine activities. You'll continue to look carefully at the way your students solve problems and have a chance to marvel at their great thinking. ▪

The Learning Environment

Working with Small Groups

In the fall, as your students finished solving a problem, you encouraged them to bring their work to you so that you could give them feedback about how well they were communicating their thinking. By now, they are probably pretty clear about what you expect of them. When you introduce a new problem, you'll want to remind them of the importance of showing their thinking. However, they should need less guidance in this. So make it clear that when they finish solving a problem during a menu time, they need to ask a classmate to check their work. Write something on the board such as, *After you've solved a problem, look it over yourself. Then ask your partner, "Can you understand how I solved this problem?"* Explain that you'll be checking their work at the end of the math period, but that you don't want to see each problem as it is solved.

Organizing Your Time

Once this process is set in motion, you're free to focus your attention on areas that you define. Maybe you want to pull students aside one by one to go over questionable solutions from the day before. Perhaps you want to work individually with a child who needs more practice with smaller numbers. Or maybe you have a small group of students who seem ready to move on to a new way of thinking if given the opportunity to try out some new ideas. These choices will depend on who your students are, and only you can judge how best to focus your attention during this time.

When the day is over, take time to look over your students' solutions to problems. Their work will help you decide who might need extra support and who can continue to work more independently. Children like to get feedback. They will appreciate having their papers returned to them marked with a simple check that shows that you have looked at their work. Papers with errors can be discussed with individuals in the spirit of "learning from mistakes."

The Mathematics

This time period will give your students a chance to do the following:

- Further develop place-value understandings by solving more of the combining and separating problems they were introduced to in the fall. The focus will be on developing efficient strategies for addition and subtraction. Efficient strategies might look like this:

$$28 + 54$$
$$20 + 50 = 70$$
$$8 + 4 = 12$$
$$70 + 12 = 82$$

or this:

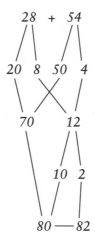

or this: •

$$28 + 54$$
$$30 + 54 = 84$$
$$84 - 2 = 82$$

- Work with the landmark number 100 and get to know their way around the 1–100 chart.
- Use their knowledge of basic facts to build connections and understanding of larger numbers. For example, a child who knows that $3 + 4 = 7$ and has developed number sense for groups of ten can make the leap to the idea that $30 + 40 = 70$.
- Try their hand at some new types of story problems that involve unknown changes (missing addends).

Protecting Students' Fragile Understandings

At about this time of year you might be tempted once again to teach the traditional algorithms of carrying and borrowing for addition and subtraction—especially to those children who haven't yet devised efficient strategies of their own. I urge you to resist this temptation. Why? The children who have not yet come up with their own efficient strategies are probably the least likely to understand these procedures. They're the ones most vulnerable to becoming confused and disheartened by rote procedures. They are unlikely to either understand or remember these methods. They are the ones who are most prone to making the errors we see so often among young children:

$$
\begin{array}{r} 28 \\ +\ 54 \\ \hline 712 \end{array}
\qquad
\begin{array}{r} 54 \\ -\ 28 \\ \hline 34 \end{array}
$$

With these students in particular, try to stay focused on what they have learned. Notice that they probably have a deep conceptual understanding of addition and subtraction and can solve problems in ways that make sense to them. They are probably still counting and may need to keep doing so. When they're exposed to more efficient methods of solving problems through class discussions and have many opportunities to solve problems, they'll begin moving on to new understandings.

Your job is to continue encouraging all students to make sense out of mathematics. Remind yourself that you have an obligation to provide many opportunities to understand our base-ten system, not rush children into procedures that cut them off from understanding. This chapter includes many such activities.

Your Textbook

If you're using a math workbook that has pages and pages of addition and subtraction problems, pick just a few of these problems and use them as a source of numbers for the story problems described below. By including these numbers when you create story problems for your students, you can honestly say that you are covering the concepts in the math book—in *great depth*.

Remind yourself that in real life, we don't encounter ready-made equations when dealing with problems. Instead, we must:

- understand the problem situation.
- choose the appropriate operation(s) and numbers to use.
- perform the operation(s).
- check to see that the answer is reasonable.

Solving pages of computation problems out of context is not going to give your students the experiences they need to succeed in life! So, keep in mind your professional obligation to teach students with methods that develop tools for lifelong learning.

Today's Number and Calendar Making

In the *Today's Number* routine, include some days when you impose rules. Try some of these ideas to encourage understanding about place value:

- Start with 100. (This rule will result in equations such as 100 + 5 + 5 + 10 + 2 = 122 and 100 + 11 + 11 = 122.)
- Use only two addends. (This will prompt students to come up with equations such as 100 + 22 and then maybe move on to 99 + 23 = 122 or 101 + 21 = 122 or even 90 + 32 = 122. Use this rule to look at number relationships, noting how one equation can lead to another.)
- Start with 200.

Also, continue to have many days when the children are allowed to follow their own interests.

And at the beginning of each month, give students time to make their calendars to take home.

Reintroducing Addition and Subtraction Problems

Start the unit off by reintroducing a combining problem one day and a separating problem the next day. Have the children visualize the action of each problem and retell the story before they go to their seats to work on the problem. Go over the importance of showing their thinking through words, numbers, and pictures.

For the *addition* problem, use numbers such as 36 + 25 in a context that students will find interesting. You might offer a bonus problem that involves the numbers 36 + 35 (or some other related equation to see if students pick up on that relationship). The bonus problem gives early finishers something to do while you meet with each child as he or she finishes the first equation. The *subtraction* problem might be 32 − 14 plus a bonus problem that includes the numbers 42 − 16.

Use these solutions as benchmarks for seeing how your students are thinking about large numbers now. Moreover, make sure to have a follow-up discussion of each problem so students can see different ways of solving them. Ask students to tell you how they solved the problem as you draw their methods on the board. You might want to start with a solution that involves direct modeling (drawing every item in the problem and counting them one by one), and then move on to a counting-up (or counting-down) solution, and then finally add some numeric solutions in which students have used chunks of numbers. (See Figure 6–1.)

It might then be appropriate to say, "Can anyone see where the numbers that Yolanda used in this solution (point to a numeric solution) are also in Marco's solution (point to a direct-modeling solution)?"

FIGURE 6–1   ▶

Students tell how they solve problems using different direct modeling, counting-up, and numeric solutions.

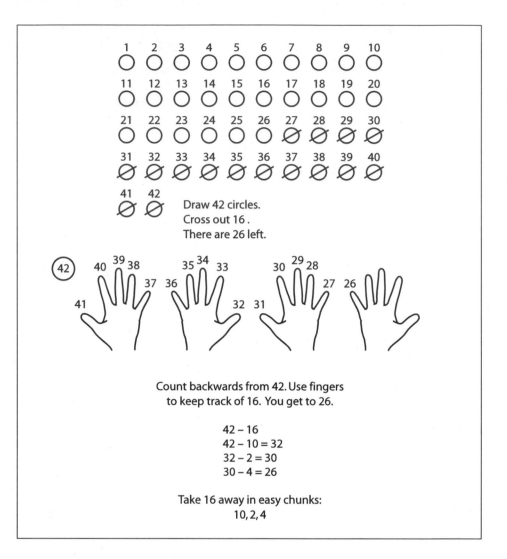

A Story-Problem Menu

To give your students lots of practice solving double-digit problems, you'll need to write some story problems yourself. These problems should:

- include both addition and subtraction scenarios.
- have numeric content that requires regrouping.
- have answers that are less than 100.
- have at least twelve different problems for the menu.

Here are some examples using simple story situations based on a class trip. Base your problems on situations familiar to your students.

If we count both our class and the other second-grade class, there were 39 children and 16 adults on the trip. How many people went to Hidden Villa from our school?

At Hidden Villa we counted 36 cherry tomatoes growing on one plant. We picked 27 of them for the students and adults from our class. How many tomatoes were left on the vine?

Students can work on these problems in any order. Remind them that you will no longer be checking each of their problems as they solve them. Encourage them to check their own work and to ask a partner to check it as well. Pick out at least one addition problem and one subtraction problem that you want everyone to do. Then have a class discussion about each of these problems. The children will gain further opportunity to hear how peers are working on problems.

Students Writing Story Problems

When your students have spent a few days working on the problems you've devised for them, introduce a new idea: "For this next set of problems, I'll supply the numbers, but you'll supply the story." After the children have written a story to go with the numbers, they will, as usual, show how they solved the problem. (See Figures 6–2, 6–3, and 6–4.)

To introduce this idea, write an equation such as *3 + 4 = 7* on the board. Ask students to think about a situation involving the equation. Have several volunteers share their ideas. If necessary, make up a story of your own to get the ball rolling. Then put another equation on the board using larger numbers, such as *17 + 8 = 25*. Repeat this process, getting lots of different

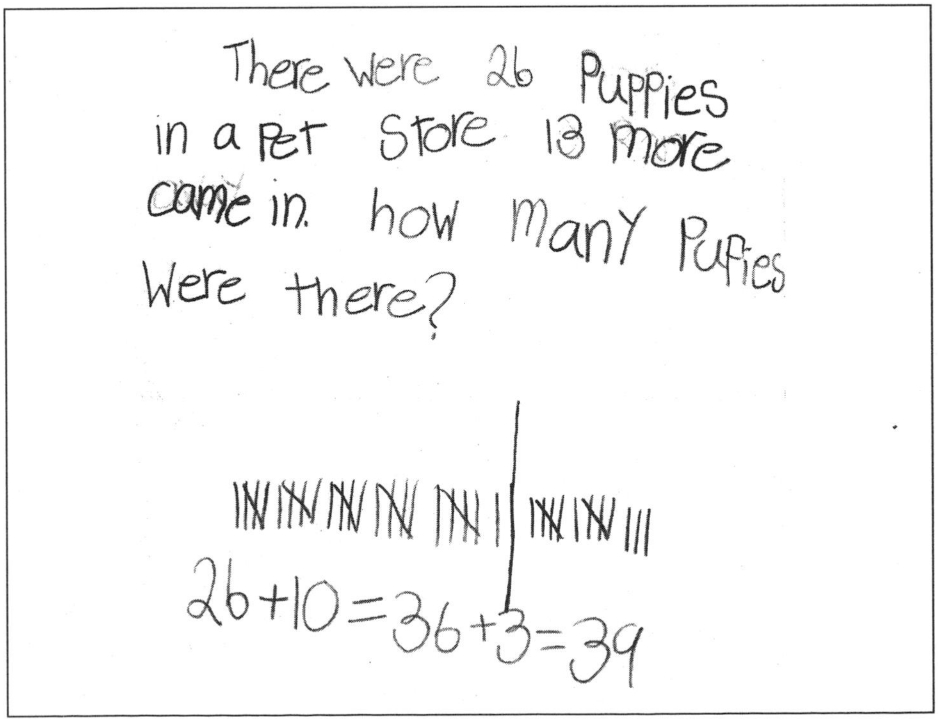

FIGURE 6–2 ◄

Katie wrote a problem for 26 + 13 and solved it two ways, with tallies and with numbers.

FIGURE 6–3 ▶

Katie used a similar
approach for 21 + 14.

there were 21 People In
the calss. and there 14
People In another calss
they whnted to be
togather In one calss
haw many People were
there?

21 + 10 = 31 + 4 = 35

14

FIGURE 6–4 ▶

Katie is comfortable sub-
tracting using a numeric
method. Her tally marks
serve as a way of illus-
trating her approach.

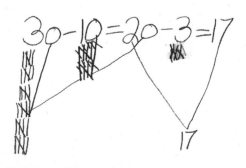

There Were 30 Kids
invited to a Birthday Party
13 Kids couldn't come how
many could come?

30 − 10 = 20 − 3 = 17

17

scenarios. Emphasize the importance of stories that are a match for the numbers.

Next write several combining and separating equations on the board. But this time, don't supply the answer. Say something like, "Today I want you to write a story that includes one of these sets of numbers. It's OK to use words or pictures to tell your story. After you've written your story, show how you solved the problem. When you finish one story, ask your partner to look at your work. Don't forget to ask, 'Can you understand my story and how I got my answer?' I'll be looking at your ideas as I circulate around the room and at the end of the period. Please don't bring your solutions to me. Just go right on to another problem when you finish one."

Exploring 100

Earlier in the year, you asked your students to get to know 10 inside and out. Now it's time to do the same thing with 100. When choosing activities, base your choices and timing on your observations of the students:

- Are the children actively engaged by the type and number of choices that you've presented? If you sense that some students are not, add more activities.

- Have you encouraged the children to plumb the mathematical possibilities inherent in an activity? Don't make the mistake of rushing. The first few times that children play a game or do an activity, they're focusing on rules and procedures. Give them time to get to the activity's mathematics. Ask good questions and show interest in their thinking as you circulate among your students, to encourage them to push for understanding.

Race for a Dollar

Coins force students to count in quantities larger than 1. And because a dime has the same value as ten pennies, working with coins helps second graders deal with the abstract notion that one thing can represent a quantity greater than 1. This activity was introduced in the fall as *Race for a Quarter*.

Materials (for each pair of children)
- no more than 30 pennies
- 5 or 6 dimes and nickels
- a few quarters

- 1 dollar bill (real or play money)
- 1 pair of dice

Instructions

This is a simple, straightforward trading game. Player 1 rolls the two dice, finds the sum of the two numbers, and takes the corresponding amount of money in coins of his or her choice. Player 1 decides if he or she wants to make any trades and then passes the dice to Player 2, who does the same thing. The first person to get coins worth $1.00 wins. You and your students can decide on the rule for ending the game. Possibilities include requiring a roll that gives the winner exactly $1.00, or a roll that gives $1.00 or more.

When you teach this game, do it slowly and thoughtfully. Demonstrate for the class how to play the game by asking a student to play it with you. As you accumulate coins, stop frequently and have the class help you compute the total value of your coins. compare your coins' current worth with the value of your opponent's coins. Muse about how far each of you is from acquiring $1.00.

It's fine to end the demonstration before either partner acquires $1.00. But take a moment and say to your students, "Does anyone know why I kept stopping and talking about the value of the coins?" If no one responds, point out that the game is fun, but that the real learning comes with understanding the value of the coins and the ways in which they compare to one another.

When playing this game, students make their own choices about when to trade coins. Typically they start by counting out the sum of the dice in pennies. Then they move on to using coins of greater value. The real challenge can lie in figuring out their total worth at any given time. You'll learn a great deal about your students as you watch them compute the value of their coins and ask them how close they are to $1.00.

Patterns on the 1–100 Chart

This activity encourages children to notice patterns on the 1–100 chart, which in turn helps them understand important relationships among larger numbers.

Materials

- a 1–100 wall chart with transparent pockets in a 10-by-10 grid
- number cards to fit in the pockets, labeled 1 to 100
- a way to highlight particular numbers (colored transparent squares work well, but you could also use colored dots or even plastic color tiles)
- a 1–100 chart (See Blackline Masters.)

1	2	3	4	5	6	7	8	9	10
11	12	13	14	15	16	17	18	19	20
21	22	23	24	25	26	27	28	29	30
31	32	33	34	35	36	37	38	39	40
41	42	43	44	45	46	47	48	49	50
51	52	53	54	55	56	57	58	59	60
61	62	63	64	65	66	67	68	69	70
71	72	73	74	75	76	77	78	79	80
81	82	83	84	85	86	87	88	89	90
91	92	93	94	95	96	97	98	99	100

Instructions

Before the lesson, insert cards 1 through 15 into the pockets of the wall chart.

Part 1: Class Lesson

Hold up one number card at a time, out of order. Ask for volunteers to come up and place the number in its appropriate pocket. Then ask the volunteers to tell how they knew where to put the particular number. It will take more than one session to fill in the whole chart. Take your time and enjoy the explanations the children offer for their choices.

Part 2: Class Lesson

Once you've constructed the whole chart, have a rule in mind that describes some of the numbers on the chart. For example:

- all the two-digit numbers that have both digits the same
- all the numbers that have at least one 3 as a digit

To introduce the game tell your rule and have your students tell you what numbers you should highlight (using colored transparent squares or another method). Once they get the basic idea of having a rule that creates a pattern on the chart, you can play without revealing the rule beforehand.

In this version, have the children guess numbers. If a number guessed by a student fits the rule, highlight it on the chart with a transparent colored square. At first their guesses will be random, but as more and more numbers that fit the rule are guessed and marked, the students should be able to make accurate guesses. Students can take turns being "it" as the class works at determining their rules.

Part 3: Individual Follow-Up—and a Menu Idea

Materials

- 1–100 chart with lines to write below (See Blackline Masters.)

Patterns on the 1–100 Chart

1	2	3	4	5	6	7	8	9	10
11	12	13	14	15	16	17	18	19	20
21	22	23	24	25	26	27	28	29	30
31	32	33	34	35	36	37	38	39	40
41	42	43	44	45	46	47	48	49	50
51	52	53	54	55	56	57	58	59	60
61	62	63	64	65	66	67	68	69	70
71	72	73	74	75	76	77	78	79	80
81	82	83	84	85	86	87	88	89	90
91	92	93	94	95	96	97	98	99	100

✂ -

Instructions

Students think of a rule and color in the numbers that fit the rule on an individual 1–100 chart. They write their rule below the chart and then give this worksheet to you. You then staple from five to ten of these completed worksheets together (with a different-color construction-paper cover for each set). Put your staples along the left-hand margin of the book, secur-

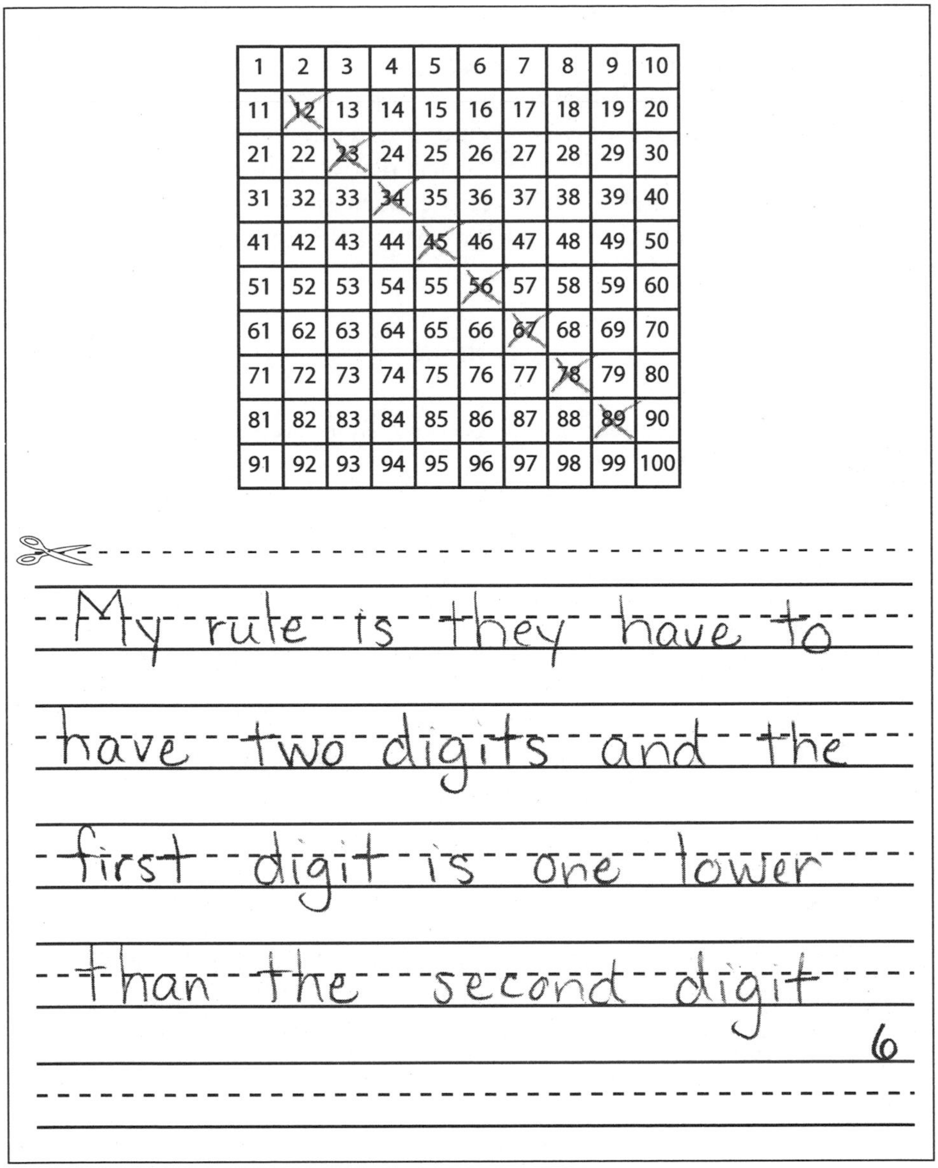

FIGURE 6–5 ◀

1	2	3	4	5	6	7	8	9	10
11	12	13	14	15	16	17	18	19	20
21	22	23	24	25	26	27	28	29	30
31	32	33	34	35	36	37	38	39	40
41	42	43	44	45	46	47	48	49	50
51	52	53	54	55	56	57	58	59	60
61	62	63	64	65	66	67	68	69	70
71	72	73	74	75	76	77	78	79	80
81	82	83	84	85	86	87	88	89	90
91	92	93	94	95	96	97	98	99	100

A child's individual pattern page. Students create a *Pattern Book* from the top portion and a corresponding *Rule Book* from the bottom portion of these types of pages.

My rule is they have to
have two digits and the
first digit is one lower
than the second digit

6

ing the book's top and bottom sections. Number the pages of each book, sequentially, at the top *and* at the bottom of each page.

Now cut *across* the book of completed worksheets, separating the 1–100 charts from the written rules. On the cover of the chart portion of the book, write *Pattern Book*. On the cover of the portion with the students' written explanations, write *Rule Book*.

As a menu activity, children can choose a number pattern that interests them from one of the *Pattern Books*, duplicate the pattern by coloring it in on a loose 1–100 chart, and then write what they think the rule is. They check their thinking against the *Rule Book* to verify their answer. (See Figure 6–5.)

Double-Digit Cover-Up

Here's a version of the *Family Math* (Stenmark, Thompson, and Cossey 1986) game *Double Digit* that involves using the 1–100 chart. After everyone has had a chance to play the game, it can become a menu item. Variations for this game are also mentioned below. Add these variations as needed to maintain interest. And see the discussions below about extending children's thinking through talking about this game.

Materials

- 1–100 chart that has squares the same size as your cubes or blocks, one per person
- 100 interlocking cubes or blocks, some snapped into rows of 10, some singles
- 1 die, to share with a partner

Instructions

Each player takes a turn rolling the dice. If the number 3 comes up, the player may take *either* three 10s *or* three single cubes to place on his or her 1–100 chart. After each player has rolled *exactly seven times,* the person who is closest to filling up the chart, without going over 100, is the winner.

This game involves skill *and* chance, taking students into the realm of probability. It also encourages estimation skills, as players decide whether to take their cubes in 1s or 10s.

Extending Thinking Through Class Discussion

Double-Digit Cover-Up also provides the opportunity for a follow-up lesson that further encourages children to use the 1–100 chart to solve addition and subtraction problems. Have this discussion after your students have played the game several times.

Begin by setting up a 1–100 chart so that everyone can see it. The chart should have the first eighty-three numbers covered. Say, "Let's pretend my chart looked like this after my first five rolls." Then ask:

"How many numbers have I covered so far?"

"How many rows of ten are covered?"

"How many ones are covered?"

After students respond, ask, "How many more cubes would I need to get exactly to one hundred? How do you know?" Although some children may tell you to count all the empty spaces one by one, listen for those who say something like, "I know it would be seven more to get to ninety and then ten more to get to a hundred." On the board, record *83 + 7 = 90* and then *90 + 10 = 100,* followed by *7 + 10 = 17.*

Another child might say, "It's ten more to get to ninety-three and then seven more to get to a hundred. This time, record *83 + 10 = 93*, and then *93 + 7 = 100*, followed by *10 + 7 = 17*.

If no one makes these kinds of suggestions, and you're sure you've provided sufficient time for students to gather their ideas together, make them yourself. Then follow up with another situation (with seventy-eight spaces covered, for example) to see if anyone picks up on your suggestions.

Extending Thinking in Small Groups

On another day, you may want to gather just a few children to discuss similar problem situations. You may choose to invite those children who typically use a counting-on, one-by-one, strategy for solving combining problems—but who you sense are on the verge of being able to use more efficient strategies.

This time give every child in the small group a board and ask them each to cover it with, say, seventy-nine cubes. Ask them how they might go about figuring out how many more cubes they need to get to 100. Say: "Write how you solved this problem. It's OK to use equations like we did yesterday on the board." As the children are working, notice how they are solving the problem. Don't discourage a one-by-one counting method. But if a child uses that method, ask him or her to find another way to check the answer. Some children need the security of knowing what an answer is before they can try out a new strategy. The 1–100 chart gives them a strong visual to rely on. And because the chart is organized in groups of ten, using it to solve this kind of problem may be just what that child needs to move on to more efficient solution strategies. You'll know if you've guessed right about your students' readiness by how they respond. If they go back to the one-by-one counting method, that's probably where they need to be—so don't push too hard on this one.

Double-Digit Variations

Variation 1—Reverse Double Digit

You can also play this game starting with a fully covered board. The object is to get as close to zero as possible. As players roll the die, they decide whether to take their roll in single cubes or rows of ten. (For example, a roll of four could result in removing four single cubes *or* four rows of ten.) Each player must roll exactly seven times.

Variation 2—Dollar Digit

Use dimes and pennies to keep track. The goal is to get as close to $1.00 without going over in exactly seven turns. Each player takes as many pennies *or* dimes as the number rolled on the dice. A player may not take both pennies and dimes on the same turn. Ten pennies can be turned in for a dime whenever a player chooses.

Variation 3—Reverse Dollar Digit

The object of the game is to end up with the least amount of money. Everyone starts with ten dimes and removes the number of dimes *or* pennies that match the roll of the dice. A player may trade in a dime for ten pennies at any time. Each player must roll exactly seven times.

Other Ideas and Resources

Repeated opportunities to play a game, along with follow-up discussions that help students deepen their understanding, are imperative to mathematical growth. So don't feel compelled to rush on to something new every day. But if you need more ideas for ways to surround your students with the concepts discussed in this chapter, two important resources are discussed below.

Teaching Arithmetic: Lessons for Addition and Subtraction, Grades 2–3 (Tank and Zolli 2001)

This book describes many games that might be especially appropriate for your class at this time of year. *Make 100* is just one of them.

Make 100

Materials

- blackboard or overhead transparency
- plain paper on which your students will draw a 4-by-4-inch grid
- partially filled grids (see below under the variation)

Instructions

Make a 4-by-4-inch grid on the chalkboard, large enough for everyone to see. Write numbers in each square so that there are number pairs adding up to 100. (See below.)

Introduce the activity by having volunteers come up and circle the pairs that add to 100. When you are sure that the students understand the game, have them create grids for one another to solve.

30	50	10	90
70	80	50	30
20	40	60	70
100	0	90	10

35	81	19	38
65	38	72	12
62	85	88	39
22	78	15	61

Variation: Have partially filled grids available. Your students must supply the missing numbers and then circle the pairs that add up to 100.

Four Strikes and You're Out

This is another favorite. It, too, requires a minimum of preparation and can be used over and over again. Here's how it works:

1. Write the digits *0* to *9* on the chalkboard.

2. Write an equation on a small piece of paper, hidden from view—one that you think would be appropriate for your students to solve; for instance, *37 + 26 = 63.*

3. Using a blank for each digit, make this template on the chalkboard: __ + __ = __.

4. Ask your students to suggest a digit. If the digit is in your equation, fill it in the appropriate spot on your template and cross the digit off your list. Your equation would look like this if someone suggested 3: 3_ + __ = _3.
   The same student keeps making guesses as long as he or she selects digits that are in the equation. If the student selects a digit that is *not* in the equation (9, for example), the class gets a "strike" and another child takes over. Use Xs to keep track of the strikes.

5. Cross out incorrect digits from your list of digits to keep track of all the numbers that have been tried so far.

Following are some examples of how the game might continue:
   Suppose that the new student suggests a 6. Now the equation looks like this: 3_ + _6 = 63. If the next guess is 1, you'd add a second strike and another student would take over. Let's say the next guess was a lucky one, 7, resulting in this 37 + _3 = 63. With the field narrowed down, the student might reason correctly that the missing digit is 2, and the class wins. If, however, the student chooses an incorrect digit, play passes to a new person and continues until there are either four strikes (in which case the equation wins) or the correct digit is chosen, resulting in a win for the class.

This game works for lots of different types of equations and can be repeated often. Make sure your template matches the equation you have in mind. For example:

_ + _ = _ _ for 2 + 8 = 10
_ _ + _ = _ _ for 14 + 7 = 21
_ _ _ − _ _ = _ _ for 100 − 25 = 75
_ + _ = _ _ for 8 + 8 = 16
_ _ + _ _ = _ _ for 35 + 29 = 64
_ _ + _ _ = _ _ _ for 22 + 78 = 100

After you've modeled playing the game a few times, invite students to submit equations for you to try out with the class. Later, they can work in pairs, devising templates and equations for each other.

Putting Together and Taking Apart: Addition and Subtraction (Russell, Economopoulos, and Wypijewski 1997)

This book is a great source of both story problems and games appropriate for second graders at this time of year. It is truly my bible for spring second graders. The following activity is just one example from the book, chosen because it's simple to describe and requires little preparation. Other activities are more elaborate, but all the materials needed to do the activities are available in the back of the book in Blackline Master form. I highly recommend this resource!

Get to 100

Materials

- 2 number cubes for every pair of students (use small blocks or blank die, on which you've marked the six faces of the cube as follows: 5, 10, 15, 20, 25, 30)
- games piece for each student, such as a cube
- a 1–100 chart for partners to share as a game board
- plain paper

Instructions

Partners take turns rolling two number cubes, finding their sum, and moving that amount on the 1–100 chart. After each roll, players record the numbers they rolled. Each new roll becomes two new addends in an addition number string. For instance, after the first roll, a person who rolled a ten and a five would write *10 + 5* and place her marker on 15. On the next roll, if she gets twenty and ten, she would have written *10 + 5 + 20 + 10* and put her marker on 45. When players make it to 100, they check their moves by adding up all the numbers. The total should equal 100:

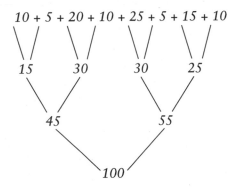

Play continues until each player reaches 100. Partners check their moves by adding up the equation that now has all the rolls that got them to 100. Partners also check each other's work to ensure there are no errors.

New Kinds of Story Problems

To have a thorough sense of addition and subtraction, students need to solve problems that involve a variety of situations. Here are some new story types that you can introduce, perhaps creating a new menu based on these opportunities and a review of old problems as well.

Problems with an Unknown Change

In real life, we sometimes have to figure out a quantity when a change has taken place. For example:

Maria had three baseball cards, and now she has ten. How many new baseball cards did she get? (3 + __ = 10)

Or:

Maria had some baseball cards. Then she got seven new baseball cards. Now she has ten. How many cards did Maria have before she got the new ones? (__ + 7 = 10)

These two examples involve *joining* two sets. You will also want your students to solve problems with an unknown change involving *separating* sets. For example:

David had ten marbles. He lost some of them. He has four marbles left. How many marbles did he lose? (10 – __ = 4)

Or:

David had some marbles. He lost six of them. Now he has four. How many did he have in the beginning? (__ – 6 = 4)

Although the equations offered for each situation represent the mathematics involved, your students may find different methods for solving these types of problems. The important thing is that each child has a method that makes sense for him or her.

When you introduce these new story situations, start with problems that involve smaller numbers. Have students visualize the action taking place, just as you did when you introduced word problems earlier in the year. Later on, you can include larger numbers for students to solve.

Remind students that they can model these problems using cubes or other counters. This kind of thinking can be very challenging for young students. They may need many opportunities to visualize the action that has taken place before they can work with the mathematics.

For a complete discussion of various types of story-problem situations, see the chapter "Addition and Subtraction" in *Math Matters: Understanding the Math You Teach* (Chapin and Johnson 2000).

Story Problems About 100

Once your students are familiar with problems that involve an unknown change, you can introduce problems that focus on the quantity 100. Some of these problems can be straightforward joining or separating situations. For example:

I had forty-five cents. I got fifty-five cents more. How much money do I have now?

I had one hundred pennies. I spent forty cents. How much money do I have left?

And now you can also include problems such as these:

I want to collect one hundred popsicle sticks for the one hundredth day of school. I have sixty-five sticks. How many more do I need to reach my goal?

Or even:

Maria and Elio want to collect one hundred popsicle sticks. Maria has thirty sticks. Elio has sixty-five. Do they have enough to reach their goal? If not, how many more do they need?

Or:

Emil had one hundred stickers. He gave some to Kenesha. Now he has eighty-eight. How many did he give to his friend.

Hitting the Wall with Subtraction

Most second graders find subtraction harder than addition. In fact, subtraction with larger numbers can become the proverbial wall that some students meet for the first time in their mathematics career. So don't be surprised if even children who have devised highly efficient strategies for adding larger numbers become less sure of themselves when solving subtraction problems. For instance, Martha had regularly solved addition problems like this:

$$29 + 45$$

$$20 \quad 9 \quad 40 \quad 5$$

$$20 + 40 = 60$$
$$9 + 5 = 14$$
$$60 + 14 = 74$$

But she initially solved subtraction problems by counting backward by ones. (See below.)

(35), 34, 33, 32, 31, 30   29, 28, 27, 26, 25   24, 23, 22, 21, 20, (19)
She counted backwards in groups of 5, using her fingers to keep track

Although Martha's method is not an efficient way to subtract, this problem solution shows a fine understanding of the problem and the operation of subtraction.

If second graders are not rushed into memorizing an algorithm they don't understand, many of them can eventually devise accurate and efficient methods that they understand. Here are some examples by second graders in late spring who were asked to first write a story problem to go with the equation 32 − 19 and then show how they would solve the problem:

Katie's Story: *"I found thirty-two stamps. Then I lost nineteen of them. How many do I have now?"*

Katie solved this problem using a strategy that involved first separating 10 from the 32 and then taking away the 9 ones:

$$32 - 10 = 22$$

$$22 - 9 = 13$$

This is the strategy I expected most students to use. But when I reviewed the rest of the papers, I found a marvelous variety of ways to think about this problem.

Ali's Story: *"There were thirty-two butterflies. Nineteen of them flew away. How many were left?"*

Ali solved this problem by decomposing the 32 into 10 + 20 + 2. Then he took the 19 away from the 20, leaving 1. Next it was a simple matter of adding the 1 to the 10 + 2 from the original 32, to come up with the correct answer of 13.

Nic's Story: *"Nic had thirty-two balloons. He gave nineteen to his sister. How many do I have?"*

Nic began by putting the 2 aside from the 30. He then did these operations:

$$30 - 10 = 20$$

$$20 - 9 = 11$$

Next he added the 2 he had put aside earlier, to get the correct answer:

$$11 + 2 = 13$$

Tom's Story: *"In school, there were thirty-two pictures on the wall. Then nineteen went home. How many pictures are on the wall?"*

Like Nic, Tom put the 2 aside from the 30. Then he did this operation:

$$30 - 9 = 21$$

Next he decomposed the 21 into 10 + 10 + 1. He had already taken 9 of the balloons away; now it was easy to take 10 more away. That left him with 10 + 1 (from the decomposed 21) + 2 (from the original 2 he had put aside). He, too, got the correct answer of 13.

Kelly's Story: *"There were thirty-two leaves on the tree. The wind blew nineteen of them off. How many were there then?"*

Kelly used these operations to solve her problem:

9 – 2 = 7

30 – 10 = 20, so

20 – 7 = 13! [The exclamation point is Kelly's.]

When I first looked at this solution, I thought Kelly's correct answer must have been a fluke. After all, a common subtraction mistake is to take the smaller number from the larger even if it is part of the minuend. Then I looked more closely and saw that Kelly's method works because she never lost track of what she was doing.

By taking the 2 from the 9, she kept in mind that she was effectively making the 32 into 30, and 19 into 17. She reduced both the minuend (32) and the subtrahend (19) by 2. Then it was a snap for her to take the 10 away to get 20 and the 7 away to get 13! (That is my exclamation point.)

I included Kelly's example because it illustrates the importance of looking carefully at what a child is doing in order to understand his or her thinking. At first, I really didn't get what Kelly was doing—and my mind didn't like it because her method wasn't *my way* of solving the problem. I understood her logical solution only when I had let go of my way of thinking about the problem. I had the same struggle with Tom's solution. Only by persisting could I follow his careful and valid line of reasoning.

Not all second graders come to such efficient and ingenious solutions when doing subtraction problems. However, I'm convinced that if we gave more children the time to develop these understandings we'd see fewer of them hitting the wall in second and third grade. It's vital to note that these solutions do not come out of thin air; rather, they stem from a deep understanding of our base-ten number system and the operation of subtraction.

Can You Subtract by Adding? Two Subtraction Models

All of the strategies above follow the take-away model of subtraction. This model involves starting with a quantity and then separating an amount from that quantity.

The comparison model, on the other hand, involves finding the difference between two quantities. Some story situations more closely fit this model.

For instance:

Mom is sixty-three inches tall, her daughter is forty-eight inches tall. How much taller is Mom?

We can solve this problem with a take-away strategy: 63 − 48 = 15. But another way to think about this situation is: 48 + __ = 63. In fact, this equation may be a more accurate representation of what is actually happening in this problem situation, and it's not unusual for children to solve this problem by starting with the smaller number and adding increments until they reach the larger number:

$$48 + 2 = 50$$

$$50 + 10 = 60$$

$$60 + 3 = 63$$

So the answer is 2 + 10 + 3 = 15.
The important thing is to let children find methods that work for them. You may want to look at the assessment in *Teaching Arithmetic: Lessons for Addition and Subtraction, Grades 2–3* (Tank and Zolli 2001), page 146, for a more complete discussion of this issue.

Other Problem-Solving Contexts

One way to give students multiple opportunities to develop efficient problem-solving strategies is to look for many different contexts. Here are a few ideas; you'll probably have many more of your own.

Lunch Count

Make up problems related to the number of kids who buy lunch each day. For example: "If there are twenty-eight students and nineteen are getting a cafeteria lunch, how many brought bag lunches?"

Calendar Date

If today is February fourteenth, how many more days are left in the month?

Today's Number

If today is the 130th day of the year, and the school year has 180 days, ask students how many more days are left in the school year.

Temperature Readings

When there's a big change in the weather, compare the temperature from a colder day to that of a warmer day. If you don't have a thermometer available, use the data from your local newspaper. If data from other cities around the world is listed in the paper, compare those temperatures with your local temperature, encouraging students to figure out the difference.

Page Numbers

If you're reading a book to the class that has ninety-five pages, and you're on page seventy-four, ask how many more pages are left in the book.

Second-Graders Count

If your class has twenty-seven kids and the other second-grade class has twenty-six, ask the class how many second graders there are at your school. Do the same computation for other grade levels. Then compare the size of the second grade with the size of the fifth grade, and so on. Ask, "Do you see any trends?"

Money: A Class Flea Market

If you're looking for a longer project, here's a motivating one for students. Have students bring in items from home that they no longer want. At the resulting flea market, the children get to "purchase" (and actually take home) items that their classmates have donated. Students are given $1.00 in play money *each time* they "shop." They have two or three chances to "buy." (Use old *Monopoly* dollars or some other duplicated form of play money that resembles a dollar bill. I like a "bill" that has George Washington's image replaced by a photo of my school principal.)

A few weeks before you plan to have your flea market, send a note home to families, asking for donations of items that a second grader might like to have—old books, toys, etc., that no longer get played with.

Sort and price the items, marking most items less than $1.00. Have real coins available at the "cashier's table" for students to use in figuring out the appropriate amount of change that a purchase might entail. Note: Change is always given in the form of a written credit. All the real money stays at the cashier's table.

Once the flea market is set up, students take turns acting as cashiers and being customers. The first time a child goes shopping, he or she is given one "dollar" to spend. The shopper and the cashier determine how much change a purchaser should be credited with, and the cashier issues a receipt for that amount. A shopper who wants to buy a big-ticket item (one that is marked over $1.00) can lay the item away and purchase it on the second round of buying—when he or she has $2.00. Students who end up with a credit at the end of the first round of purchasing can add that amount to the new dollar they get for their second round.

After two or three rounds of buying, all unused credit is returned to the "bank" and unpurchased items can be donated to a local charity (or discreetly placed in the trash).

And so on

Keep your eyes open for opportunities to add and subtract numbers that are meaningful to your students. We all get better at skills when we have a chance to practice them. Using the same skill in many different contexts can keep the work fresh and interesting.

Helping Parents Understand

You'll want parents to understand and support what you're doing in the classroom. If you didn't send home the parent letter from Chapter 3 earlier in the year, this is the time to do it. If you sent that letter home earlier, update it, based on what you see your students doing now, and send it again.

Assessing Growth

Figures 6–6 through 6–9 show simple assessments to use at the end of this unit. (See also Blackline Masters.)

By the time you introduce these assessments, your students will have had many opportunities to write and solve story problems of this nature, so the introductions can be brief. Do the addition problem one day and the subtraction problem on another. When assessing ability, look for these benchmarks:

- students who still need to count to solve the problem
- students who can use a counting on strategy
- students who have a numeric solution that involves using groups of 10

Again, don't be surprised if you see more efficient work in addition than in subtraction.

Story Problems

16 + 35

Write your story problem here:

Thir was 16 compruters in a
Stor. amd they got ℰ5 mor
compeuters. Th

Using words, pictures, numbers and other symbols,   solve your
story problem:

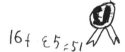

16+ ℰ5 = 51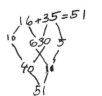

FIGURE 6–6 ◀

Martin wrote a story that matched the addition expression and then solved the problem accurately by creating a direct model of the problem, drawing one square for each of the computers. His work shows understanding of a combination situation, but his solution requires counting, an inefficient strategy.

Story Problems

16 + 35

Write your story problem here: Once upon a time
there was a girl she had a stamp calecshin.
She had 16 stamps she got 35 more
how much did she have?

Using words, pictures, numbers and other symbols,   solve your
story problem:

16+35=51   16+35=51
   10 630 5   10+30=40
      40   40+6=46
      51   46+5=51

FIGURE 6–7 ◀

Maddy was able to make a story to match the addition expression and then found two slightly different ways to solve the problem by decomposing the numbers into 10s and 1s to make them easier to combine.

FIGURE 6–8 ▶

Aaron wrote a subtraction story that matched the subtraction expression and then decomposed the number 19 into 10 and 9, creating easy-to-subtract chunks.

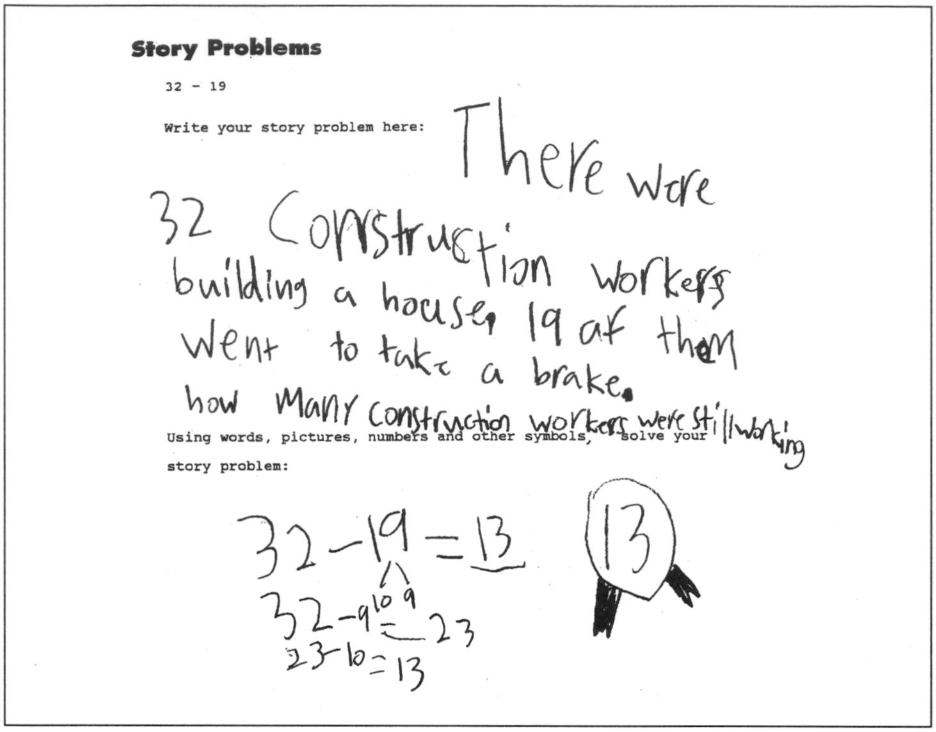

Story Problems

32 - 19

Write your story problem here: There were 32 Construction workers building a house, 19 of them went to take a brake.

Using words, pictures, numbers and other symbols, how many construction workers were still working solve your story problem:

$$32 - 19 = 13$$

$$32 - 9^{10 \; 9} = 23$$

$$23 - 10 = 13$$

⑬

FIGURE 6–9 ▶

Flora solved the subtraction problem in three ways: decomposed both numbers into 1s and 10s; counted backwards from 32; and changed 19 to the friendly number 20. Her multiple strategies show excellent number sense.

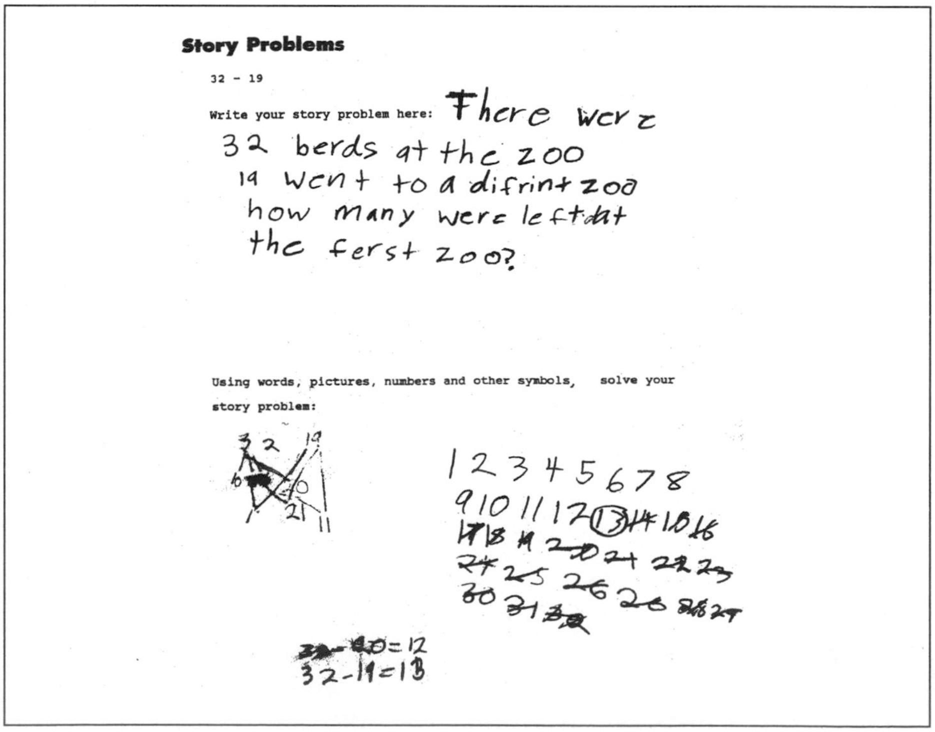

Story Problems

32 - 19

Write your story problem here: There werz 32 berds at the zoo 19 went to a difrint zoo how many were left dat the ferst zoo?

Using words, pictures, numbers and other symbols,   solve your story problem:

1 2 3 4 5 6 7 8
9 10 11 12 13 14 15 16
17 18 19 20 21 22 23
24 25 26 27 28 29
30 31 32

$$32 - 20 = 12$$

$$32 - 19 = 13$$

Chapter 7

April

TAKING STOCK

In April, it's time to take stock of what you and your students have accomplished this year and think through what you hope to present to the class during the remaining months. Only you can decide what direction to take with your class. You may want to spend this month finishing up addition and subtraction work. Giving students ample time to explore mathematical concepts is key to developing lasting understanding. Base your decisions for April primarily on what you think would be most useful to your students. But also review your local standards to see if they suggest a helpful direction in which to move.

If students are ready for something new, consider introducing multiplication this month; use the categorical-data-collection unit described in the December chapter, or try a unit on numeric data collection. Or head in a different direction—one that involves integrating mathematics with other curricular areas. For example, creating a model village can bring together math, literature, and social studies in fun and satisfying way.

Sharing the village with parents adds to the children's sense of accomplishment. Some suggestions for these activities are listed later in this chapter.

During April, you and your students may also have to hunker down and prepare for taking a standardized test. If that is your fate, you may want to skip now to the section of this book on test preparation (see page 179). ■

The Learning Environment

Whatever academic direction you take, you may notice a subtle social change in your second graders at this time of year. In the spring, second graders often start to feel "too big" for second grade. They're less interested in pleasing their teachers and more interested in each other. This shift in focus can be disconcerting to a teacher. Knowing that this change is typical for second graders in the spring can take some of the sting out of the situation. This new "outward-looking" attitude is not a rejection of you personally, but a sign that your students are growing up. They need opportunities to exercise their growing maturity with more and more opportunities to make good decisions and take responsibility for their learning.

The Mathematics

Today's Number and Calendar Making

Sometime this month, use the daily *Today's Number* routine as an opportunity to introduce the vertical way of writing equations. For example, if a child says "ninety plus forty-five," instead of using the usual horizontal format, $90 + 45 = 135$, record the equation using a vertical format:

$$\begin{array}{r} 90 \\ +\ 45 \\ \hline 135 \end{array}$$

Say, "Here's another way to record Brendan's idea with mathematical symbols. It's just another way of saying when you add ninety to forty-five you have a total of one hundred and thirty-five. Who can prove that this equation works?"

A student will likely say something like, "I added the ninety and the forty. That made one hundred and thirty. I know because I took one of the tens from the forty and gave it to the ninety to make one hundred. I took the thirty that was left after I took the ten away from the forty, and added it to the one hundred. Then I still have five left, so I added that to the one hundred and thirty. That gives me one hundred and thirty-five. Another child may have another equally efficient method of proving the equation.

Your students' methods probably will not include the standard borrowing and carrying algorithm, because they have no need for it even when a vertical format is used to record an equation.

Continue the discussion by recording another equation, perhaps one with three addends, in the vertical format. Help your students to understand that in order to solve the problem, they would need to add all three numbers together. Listen to their ideas of how they might accomplish this task.

Use the horizontal format to record most equations—it allows children to focus more easily on the quantities represented by the symbols. Occasionally, however, use the vertical format so your students become familiar with it.

Don't forget to have your students make an April calendar early in the month.

An Introduction to Multiplication

Some of your students may have already experimented with multiplication when writing their *Today's Number* equations. For instance, one day in my class, Edwin offered this equation:

$$(4 \times 13) + (3 \times 5) = 67$$

I knew that the other children might have trouble proving this one, so I asked Edwin to tell us how he figured out what 4×13 was. He answered that he didn't really know the answer to that part of the equation, but that he was pretty sure the equation worked. He went on to say that he started with the equation $15 + 15 + 15 + 15 + 7 = 67$. He then decomposed all the fifteens to make this equation: $7 + 8 + 7 + 8 + 7 + 8 + 7 + 8 + 7 = 67$. From that equation he decided to decompose the 7s and 8s still further:

$$3 + 4 + 4 + 4 + 3 + 4 + 4 + 4 + 3 +$$
$$4 + 4 + 4 + 3 + 4 + 4 + 4 + 3 + 4 = 67$$

"And that's how I know my equation is correct," he said. "I counted all the fours and found out there were thirteen, so I said four times thirteen—because that's the same as thirteen times four—and then I did the same thing with the threes. There were five of them, so I wrote three times five. That's how I know my equation works."

Edwin's method shows a deep understanding of multiplication as repeated addition—one of the big ideas in multiplication. It also shows how inventive students can be when they are given the opportunity to think deeply about number!

Second graders often view multiplication as a "grown-up" skill, and they can be very motivated to learn more about it. Note that quick recall of the single-digit multiplication facts is not a second-grade skill. That task is much more realistic for older students. However, second graders can begin to develop a conceptual understanding of multiplication. In fact, they often find that multiplication is a better intellectual match for them than is subtraction of larger numbers. Multiplication is closely related to addition and, unlike subtraction, does not involve thinking in reverse.

The focus in multiplication should be on:

- helping students see the connection between repeated addition (the concept that $2 + 2 + 2 = 6$ is the same thing as $3 \times 2 = 6$).
- giving students chances to see and use different visual models of multiplication.
- developing language that helps students connect the concept of multiplication with the appropriate mathematical symbols.

How Many Feet in Our Class Today?
Things That Come in Groups

Here's a problem that gets children thinking about adding equal-sized groups.

Begin by asking the children to figure out how many feet (or legs, or eyes, or ears) there would be if four students were sitting at one of the tables in the room. Have volunteers explain their reasoning. You're likely to hear suggestions such as counting by twos around the table, or one of the following equations: $2 + 2 + 2 + 2 = 8$, or $4 + 4 = 8$. Then pose a larger problem: "How many feet are in the class altogether today?" Determine the number of people who are present and then remind the children that you want them to use words, pictures, numbers, or other symbols to show how they got their answers. Give the children time to work as you circulate, noting the different methods used. Later that day or on the next day, have the children share their methods of determining the number of feet. Figures 7–1 and 7–2 show some typical second-grade responses.

Use this discussion to make the point that multiplication is a fast way to figure out how many you have when you have many groups that are all the same size, as Edwin has shown in his work in Figure 7–2. Also, ask the children to think about other things that come in groups of twos. These might include eyes, ears, shoes, and wheels on a bicycle. List these on the board. Then create lists of things that come in threes, fours, fives, and sixes. You might have lists that look something the one in Figure 7–3 on page 164.

Explain that you'll be transferring these lists to large pieces of paper so that students can add new ideas as they come up with them. You'll use these lists to do the *Patterns in Multiples* activity described on page 167.

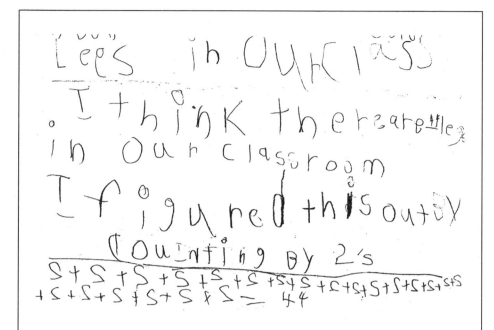

Lees in OUR CLASS
. I think ther are tile
in Our classroom
I figured this out by
Counting by 2's
5+5+5+2+5+5+5+5+5+5+5+5+5+5+5
+5+5+5+5+5+5 — 2+5 — 44

FIGURE 7–1 ◄

**Howard drew 22 twos
and then used them to
count to 44 by twos.**

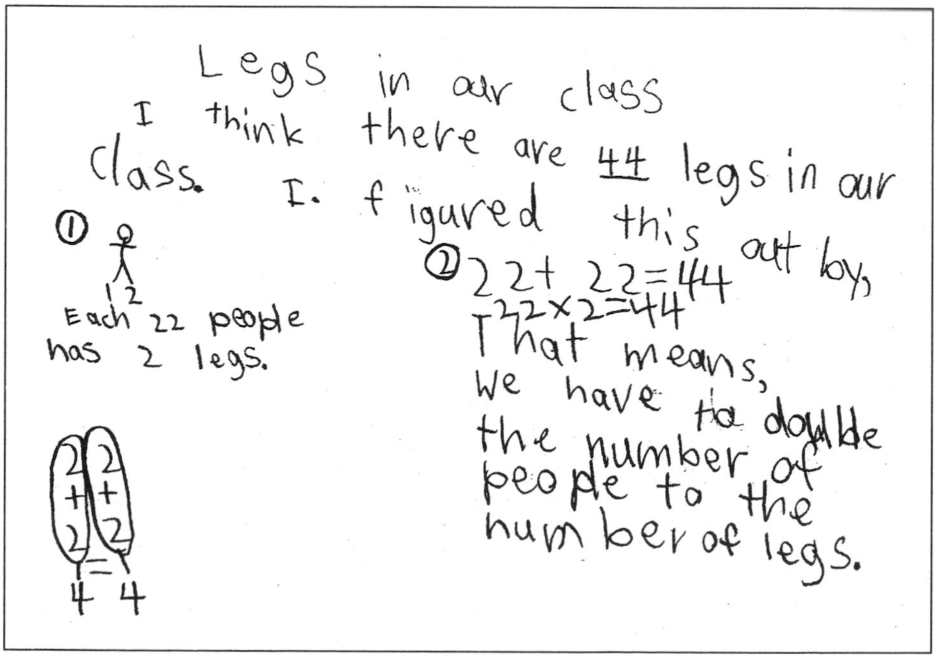

Legs in our class
I think there are 44 legs in our
class. I figured this out by,
① Each 22 people has 2 legs.

② 22+22=44
22×2=44
That means,
we have to double
the number of
people to the
number of legs.

2 2
+ +
2 2
— —
4 4

FIGURE 7–2 ◄

**Edwin got his answer by
doubling 22.**

FIGURE 7–3 ▶

Things that come in groups.

Things That Come in Groups

2s
eyes
ears
shoes
wheels on a bicycle

3s
wheels on a tricycle
corners on a triangle

4s
wheels on a car
corners on a square

5s
points on some stars
fingers on one hand
toes on one foot

6s
legs on an insect
points on a star of David

Circles and Stars

This activity provides a strong visual interpretation of multiplication as repeated addition. It is a fine way to introduce the language and symbols of multiplication, and is described more fully in the book *Teaching Arithmetic: Lessons for Introducing Multiplication, Grade 3* by Marilyn Burns (2001). The following lesson is a pared-down version of the original and is suitable for second graders.

Materials

- 1 die for every 2 students
- $8\frac{1}{2}$-by-11-inch paper for every student

Instructions

1. Teach the game by playing it with the class as your opponent. You'll need one die and the chalkboard. Have a piece of $8\frac{1}{2}$-by-11-inch paper on hand to show the children how to fold their paper into quarters to make a place to record four rounds of the game. Divide the chalkboard into two sections—one for you to draw your circles and stars on, and one to record the class's work.

2. Explain that you'll roll the die once to determine how many *circles* to write on your side of the board. If you roll a three, draw three large circles on your side of the board. Roll again and let the children know that this second roll tells you how many *stars* to put in *each* circle. If you roll a four on your second roll, your side of the board would look like this:

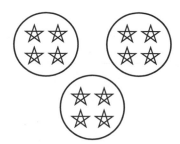

3. Say, "That's why we call the game *Circles and Stars*. The first roll tells how many circles to make, the second roll tells how many stars to put in each circle. Now I have to figure out how many stars I have altogether. Who has an idea what three groups of four is altogether?" Take suggestions from your students and then write your total for this round.

4. Now ask a student to roll once to determine the number of circles to draw on the other side of the chalkboard. Then ask someone else to roll again to determine the number of stars. Have volunteers suggest ways to figure out the total number of stars that the class has accumulated.

5. If you feel that the children understand the basics of the game, demonstrate folding an $8\frac{1}{2}$-by-11-inch piece of paper into quarters, and explain that partners will now play the game with each other, playing four rounds. For each round, players should figure out their total number of stars. When all four rounds are over, each player should determine the grand total number of stars he or she has accumulated. A finished paper would look like Figure 7–4.

6. After the children have all played four rounds of the game (perhaps on Day 2), have a class discussion about their results. You might ask questions such as:

> "What was the greatest number of stars you got in one round?"
>
> "Did anyone get more than thirty-six?"
>
> "How did you get thirty-six? So, when you get six groups of six, your score is thirty-six. Is there another way to get thirty-six?"
>
> "What was the least number?"
>
> "Did anyone get twelve stars? If so, what did your paper look like? Did anyone get twelve stars in a different way?"
>
> "Did anyone get seven stars in one round? Why not?"

As the children respond to your questions, use the language "two groups of four give you eight stars" or "two sets of four is eight altogether."

FIGURE 7–4 ▶

**Joelle had thirty-four
stars after four rounds.**

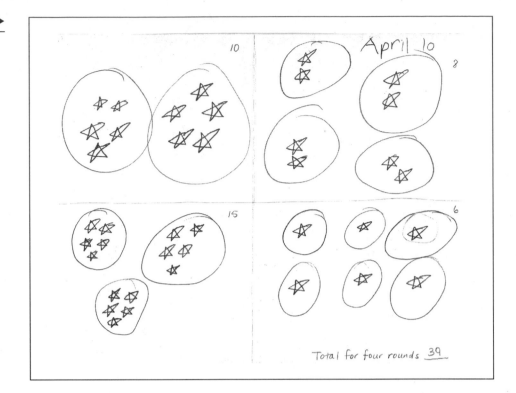

7. On the board draw three circles with four stars in each one and label
it in three ways:

   ■ 3 groups of 4 is 12

   ■ 3 sets of 4 is 12

   ■ 3 × 4 = 12

   Explain that the × is the mathematical symbol that means *groups
of* or *sets of*. Say, "Now I'd like you to use one or more of these ways
to label each of your rounds for the game. Use the language that makes
the most sense to you. When you finish, turn your paper over and play
four more rounds with your partner. Again, label each round with at
least one of these ways for describing your circles and stars and totals."

8. On future days, encourage students to keep playing *Circles and Stars*
at school and at home.

What Makes a Good Shape for a Quilt?

Materials

   ■ 4 6-by-6-inch construction-paper squares for the class demonstration

   ■ color tiles for your students, 24 for each pair

■ grid paper, the same size as your color tiles

Instructions

1. This activity introduces a geometric model for multiplication. Gather your students on the rug in a circle. Explain that you are working on a quilt made of square blocks and want to figure out a good shape for the finished quilt. Display four 6-by-6 squares of construction paper. Ask if anyone has an idea how you might arrange the squares to make a rectangular-shaped quilt.

2. Rearrange the squares according to your students' suggestions, using the language of "one by four" and "two by two." Write these ideas as 1×4, and 2×2 on the chalkboard.

3. Now explain that the kids' assignment is to figure out all the rectangular quilts that can be made with six squares, with twelve squares, and with twenty-four squares. Say: "You'll be using color tiles to try out all the possibilities. I'd like you to record each of the rectangles you make by cutting out the rectangles using the grid paper. Make sure to label each rectangle."

4. After the children have had a chance to work on the problem, bring them together to discuss their findings and to share their ideas about which rectangles they think would be most suitable for a quilt.

   If you wish to extend your students' opportunity to work with a geometric model of multiplication, partners can choose other numbers of tiles to work with. For example, they might explore which of the numbers from 1 to 24 can be made into many different possible rectangles. Ask, "Are there some numbers that can only be arranged to form one rectangular array?"

Patterns in Multiples

Again, for a fuller description of this activity, see *Teaching Arithmetic: Lessons for Introducing Multiplication, Grade 3* (Burns 2001).

Materials

■ The *Things That Come in Groups* chart, generated by the class earlier
■ 1–100 charts, 1 per student
■ counters

Instructions

This activity encourages second graders to examine the patterns in multiples for numbers 2 through 6. It's also an opportunity to introduce a

T-chart as a way of keeping track of information and mathematical relationships.

1. Remind the students that they recently talked about the number of feet that four people have. Tell the class that today you're going to think about the number of *ears* that four people have.

2. Ask four students to come to the front of the room, and count their ears by ones and twos.

3. Write the equation $4 \times 2 = 8$ on the board and remind the class that this equation is for a total of eight ears.

4. Now ask, "How many ears do six people have?"

5. Have two more students come up so that the class can confirm their thinking. Write on the board: $6 \times 2 = 12$

6. Explain that "now I'm going to make a list that shows how many ears there are for one person, two people, three people, and so on." As you write the following information on the board, encourage the children to help you come up with the correct number of ears for the number of people:

People	Ears	
1	2	$1 \times 2 = 2$
2	4	$2 \times 2 = 4$
3	6	$3 \times 2 = 6$
4	8	$4 \times 2 = 8$
5	10	$5 \times 2 = 10$
6	12	$6 \times 2 = 12$

7. Next, show how you can record on a 1–100 chart a pattern for the number of ears. (See Figure 7–5.)

8. Explain that partners will work together to choose one item from the *Things That Come in Groups* chart. Their job will be to generate a T-chart for the item, showing all the multiples for that item, from 1 through 6. For example, if they decide to do wheels on a tricycle, they should show how many wheels one tricycle has, how many wheels two tricycles have, and so on, up to the number of wheels for six tricycles. They should then color in the multiples on a 1–100 chart, just as you did for the ears.

   Figuring out the multiples for numbers by 3, 4, and 6 can prove challenging for second graders. Make sure your students know that they can use counters to accomplish this task. Invite them to use the 1–100 chart itself to count out the multiples.

FIGURE 7–5 ◀

On this chart, the multi-
ples of 2 have been
shaded.

1	2	3	4	5	6	7	8	9	10
11	12	13	14	15	16	17	18	19	20
21	22	23	24	25	26	27	28	29	30
31	32	33	34	35	36	37	38	39	40
41	42	43	44	45	46	47	48	49	50
51	52	53	54	55	56	57	58	59	60
61	62	63	64	65	66	67	68	69	70
71	72	73	74	75	76	77	78	79	80
81	82	83	84	85	86	87	88	89	90
91	92	93	94	95	96	97	98	99	100

Partners who finish early can choose a second item from the list
and generate both a T-chart and color in a 1–100 chart for that second item.

9. Display the colored 1–100 charts and give your students a chance to
   notice the different patterns that emerge on the charts.

The activities listed above will give your students a start on understanding
multiplication. When they encounter multiplication again in third grade,
they may have a level of comfort and understanding that allows them to
delve more deeply into the topic, with greater confidence.

Numeric-Data Collection

The graphing choices suggested in Chapter 4 generally involved collecting
categorical data. Students were asked to think about which group they
belonged to. For example, "What month were you born in? How did you
get to school—walk, car, bus, bicycle? Are you the oldest, youngest, middle, or only child in your family?"

Numeric data has a different slant. It answers questions about *how many*.
For instance, "How old are you? How many blocks is your home from
the school? How many people are in your family?" When focusing on
numeric data, you'll first want to provide your students with a model by
choosing an interesting question to investigate as a class. Later, you'll set

them free to pursue their own investigations. And make sure your class investigation gives students practice collecting, organizing, representing, and analyzing data. Ideally, new questions leading to further investigation will grow out of this analysis.

A Numeric-Data-Collection Experience, Based on *The Story of Z*

Instructions

1. To prepare for the larger investigation described below, make a class graph that answers the question, "How many letters in our names?" Each child writes his or her name, one letter at a time, on a strip of 1-inch graph paper. Cut off any empty cells so the length of the names can be easily seen. Create this simple graph by setting up one column for all the names that have 2 letters, another column for those that have 3 letters, etc. (See Figure 7–6.)

2. Once the data is organized, ask students what they notice about the data. Examples of their responses might include:

   - There are more people who have five letters in their names.
   - Only one person has two letters.
   - The longest name has seven letters.

3. Later, read *The Story of Z* by Jeanne Mod (1990). This tale involves an altercation that takes place among the letters of the alphabet when the letter Z becomes convinced that she is underutilized and underappreciated. Second graders delight in Z's huffiness and love the spelling problems that result from her defection (*ip up your ippers, the ebras at the oo*).

4. After reading the story, ask students, "I wonder if Z is correct. We know she's last in the alphabet, but is she really the letter that is used least? How could we use our name graph to find out?" If no one suggests it, explain that you could arrange the same data collected in the earlier graph in a different format. For this graph, you'll have each person in the class cut on the lines between each letter of his or her name. Then the class can put all the As together in one column, have another column for all the Bs, and so on through the alphabet. Say: "This new format will help us see how many times each letter of the alphabet is used for spelling all our first names. We should be able to see which letters are used less often in our names."

   If you can't get a copy of *The Story of Z,* just pose another question such as, "I wonder which letter is used most when we write all

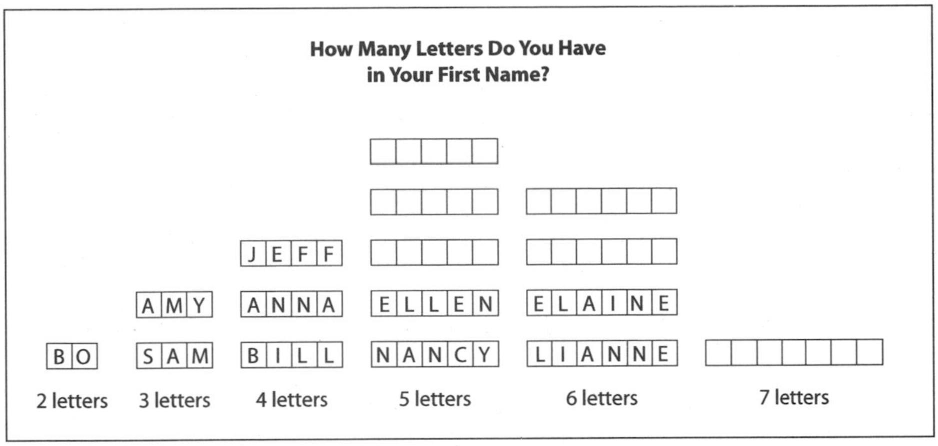

FIGURE 7–6 ◀

How Many Letters Do You Have in Your First Name?

| 2 letters | 3 letters | 4 letters | 5 letters | 6 letters | 7 letters |

Children create a graph based on the number of letters in their first names.

of our first names?" Then go on to discuss a new way of representing the data so you can answer this new question.

5. Show the chart you've prepared with the letters of the alphabet listed in a column down the left-hand side of a large piece of paper. Explain that this time they'll be gluing their letters down one at a time. Ask students to write their names on a new piece of 1-inch graph paper and then to cut the letters apart. While the class is pursuing some independent activity (silent reading, playing a math game, etc.), have a few students at a time add the letters of their first names to this new graph next to the corresponding letter. (See Figure 7–7.)

6. When the graph is complete and it's convenient to do so, ask students to describe what they notice about this graph. For example:

"Does this graph support Z's concerns?"

"What else does this graph show us?" (There are likely to be lots of As and Es on this graph—ask why that is so.)

"How is this graph different from our original names graph?"

"Why does this graph look so different, if both graphs have the same information (all the letters in our names)?"

You can use these two representations to illustrate how the same data, arranged differently, can tell very different stories!

7. There are many directions you could go in now. Here are some possibilities:

"Which graph would be most helpful to us if we wanted to find out how many letters there are altogether in our first names? Would we get the same or different answers from counting each of the letters in the two graphs?"

FIGURE 7–7 ▶

Children create a graph to figure out how many times each letter of the alphabet is used for spelling their first names.

A	a	a	A	a	a	
B	B	B				
C	c					
D						
E	e	e	E	e	E	e
F	f	f				
G						
H						
I	i	i	i			
J	J					
K						
L	l	l	L	l	l	l
M	m	m				
N	N	n	n	n	n	n
O	o					
P						
Q						
R						
S	S					
T						
U						
V						
W						
X						
Y	y	y				
Z						

"How would a graph of the letters in our last name compare to the graph of letters in our first names? What if we just graphed our initials?"

"Getting back to Z's original concern about being the least-used letter of the alphabet, is there any other group of letters that you might want to graph?" (You might want to choose a sentence or two from a favorite story and graph the letters used in it.)

8. Once you've exhausted your students' interest in this investigation, let them pursue questions involving numeric-data investigations of their own. Explain that they'll be collecting data from their classmates on a topic that interests them. Start by making a class list of questions that could be investigated. For example:

"How many pets do you have?"

"How many times can you write your name in one minute?"

"How many times have you been to the zoo?"

Let your students know that they'll have about four class math periods in which to choose a question, collect the data, organize and represent the information, and finally analyze it so it can be presented to the class. Decide if you want your students working individually or with partners. Before the children begin working, spend a few moments discussing the importance of thoughtful work. Ask how that might look as people move about the room collecting data from one another.

9. Have a stack of class lists available for those who want to use the list to keep track of their data. By the end of the first day, explain that each person (or pair) needs to turn in a paper with the question they plan to ask their fellow students and a plan for what they will do each day. For example, they might write:

> We're going to ask everyone how many teeth they've lost.
>
> On Tuesday we'll collect the data.
>
> On Wednesday we'll decide how to organize the data and start to draw it.
>
> On Thursday we'll finish drawing and think about what we'll say to the class.

10. Once the children begin working, circulate as they make and carry out their plans during the next few days.

11. On the fifth day, give students a few minutes to practice what they plan to tell the class about their investigations. Then bring the class together to share.

For other ideas on collecting and representing numeric data, see *How Many Pockets? How Many Teeth?* (Wright 1997). This is an excellent second-grade resource for collecting and representing numeric data.

Gingerbread Village

The project described below is a shortened version of *The Gingerbread Village* in the book *Math Excursions 2* (Burk, Snider, and Symonds 1991). This version takes at least a week to complete. It also requires planning to ensure that you have enough half-gallon milk cartons for all the buildings in the village.

Materials

- 1 half-gallon milk carton for each child for their house
- up to 4 cartons for every 2 children for the village building they choose to make
- utility knives—to be wielded by *adults only*
- scissors for the children

- gesso paint for an undercoat on the buildings to make the tempera paint stick
- tempera paint
- 4-by-4-inch squares of construction paper in two shades of green (for grass), brown (for parking lots), and black (for streets)
- 32-by-32-inch squares of paper, 1 for every 4 students
- construction paper, shades of green tissue paper, popsicle sticks, and modeling clay to make people, trees, and other items for the village.

Instructions

Preparation

Begin this unit by telling your own version of *The Gingerbread Boy* (or Girl!)—but stop short of the fatal ending in which the fox snaps up the main character. Instead, describe how the boy or girl (or both of them) manages to escape across the river only to find a fabulous village peopled by other escaped gingerbread characters. After the recent escapees have a chance to marvel at the wonderful place, a village elder explains the building codes that have governed the construction of the village. Explain that the class will be using these codes to build a gingerbread village of their own in the classroom.

The codes are:

- The town must be built in sections. Four people must work together on each section. The sections measure 32 by 32 inches.
- Each section may have up to four houses and one or two additional buildings.
- Houses must be the size of one half-gallon milk carton; other buildings may be up to four milk cartons in size.
- Every milk carton will be allotted four 4-by-4-inch squares of land. These squares must be arranged in rectangles. (Square or oblong rectangles are acceptable.)
- Streets may be only one square wide but as long as needed.
- Any land not covered by building lots and streets must be used as open space in the form of parks.
- A town-hall meeting must be held before construction begins, to determine what buildings are needed to serve the town and how large each building shall be.

Town Meeting

To get started on the village, you'll need to schedule the town-hall meeting. Start by brainstorming a list of possible buildings for the village. This discussion gives students an opportunity to examine what goods and services a community needs. Keep in mind that no section can have more than two additional buildings and that four people are needed to work on each section. You and your class will also have to figure out the total number of buildings possible for your class to build. (For instance, a class of twenty will build five sections, allowing for only ten buildings to house goods and services.) This may require some winnowing down of the original list of possibilities. You may need to vote after individuals have made their cases about why a particular building is necessary.

Other decisions you'll need to make include deciding how many cartons to use for each building, which set of partners will make each of the chosen buildings, and how to form groups of four for the section building.

Designing the Houses

Once all of these decisions are made, you can begin building. The original unit includes designing and decorating the interior and exteriors of the houses, but you may want to limit your students to working on their homes' exteriors. They can choose how to orient their milk cartons (see Figure 7–8), and begin drawing where they want windows and doors to be on their homes. Consider having an extra adult or two around, with utility knives in hand, to help the children make the openings. Students should be able to complete the cutting with scissors once a slit has been cut into the carton.

Painting the Houses

Many milk cartons resist tempera paint, so have gesso available to prime the surface. Once the gesso has dried, the children can paint the exterior of their homes.

FIGURE 7–8 ◀

Different ways to orient milk cartons to build houses.

A house can be made from an upright carton …

Or the carton can be placed on it's side …

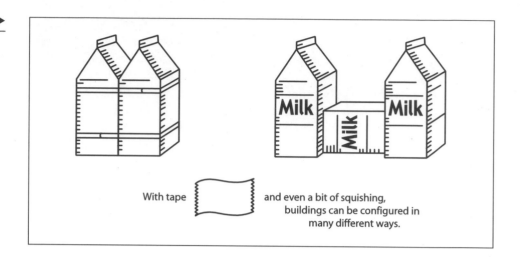

With tape and even a bit of squishing, buildings can be configured in many different ways.

Making the Buildings

Next, students construct the buildings discussed and chosen in the town-hall meeting. Make masking tape available to the children and encourage them to think through many possible ways to orient their cartons in relationship to one another as they construct their buildings. (See Figure 7–9.) Once the cartons are taped together, follow the same procedure for creating openings and painting the buildings. You may want to put some thought into adding signs to the completed buildings.

Creating the Sections

By working in a group of four to lay out a section of the village, the children have a wonderful opportunity to engage in spatial problem solving. Review the building codes so the students have a chance to think through how many squares they will need for each building. Discuss how each house will need four light green squares. Look at the two potential arrangements of these four squares, given the requirement that plots of land must be rectangular in shape. (See below.)

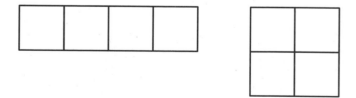

Go on to discuss the number of green and brown squares that each building will need, depending on the number of cartons used to create the building. Buildings made of two cartons, for instance, are allotted eight squares. These can be a combination of green squares for "landscaped"

areas and brown squares for parking lots. Also review the code that limits streets to a width of one square but allows them to be as long as needed to serve the buildings.

Once the children have these ideas firmly in mind, they can start working on placing the 4-by-4-inch green, brown, and black squares onto the 32-by-32-inch square of paper. While they are working, circulate among them, reminding them of the building codes and supporting them as they problem solve. Also remind them that any space not used for buildings and streets can be covered with more dark green squares for neighborhood parks. As groups finish their arrangements, they can work together to glue the squares down. (See Figure 7–10.)

Putting the Village Together

When all of the sections are complete, call another town-hall meeting to decide how the town sections should be arranged. You may want to have some long strips of black paper (4 inches wide) to serve as streets between the various sections, to ease the flow of traffic. See Figure 7–11 for a completed village plan.

Populating the Village

Once the sections are attached to one another and placed in the space you've set aside to display the village, the children can take turns putting their houses and buildings in place. When they have finished this task, give them time to make "gingerbread" people out of paper. You might suggest that they can make their characters stand up by gluing them to popsicle sticks held up by a small ball of clay. If your students make a back and front for

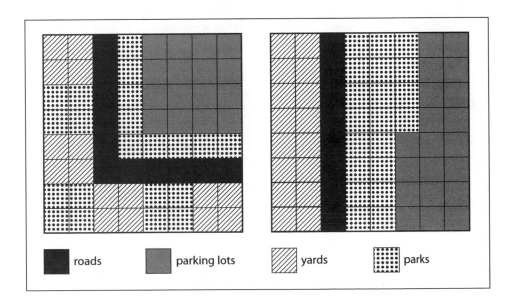

FIGURE 7–10 ◄

Children decide how to arrange their villages on large squares of paper.

FIGURE 7–11 ▶

Use 4" strips of black paper between sections to create connected streets, easing traffic flow.

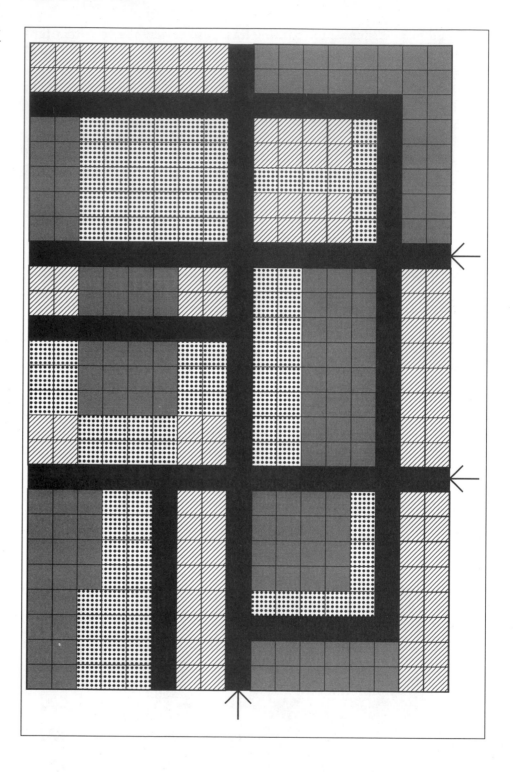

their people, the stick disappears. The youngsters can use their ingenuity to come up with ways to make trees, bushes, stop signs, crosswalks, lakes for the parks, etc.

This is a great spring unit for second graders and will leave them feeling proud of their accomplishment. Invite other classes or parents to enjoy the finished project.

Standardized-Test Preparation

Easing Anxiety

High-stakes tests almost invariably create anxiety on the part of teachers and administrators. If you are required to administer a standardized test this month, try not to communicate this anxiety to your students. Do honestly answer questions students have about the test. During this discussion, assure the children that the test will *not* determine whether they go on to third grade next year (unless it will). Explain that no one is expected to get all the answers correct on a standardized test. (With the ambiguity inherent in most standardized tests, you can probably honestly state that even *you* would have a hard time answering all the questions correctly.) Assure students that it's possible to miss items on the test and still do very well. Helping your students relax about these issues gives them a better chance of doing their best on the test.

On testing days, make sure your classroom is physically comfortable. Classrooms that are too hot or too cold or plagued by extraneous distractions such as outside noise can limit your students' ability to concentrate. On testing days, make the rest of the planned activities undemanding, and call a halt to homework during the testing period. You can't control when your students go to bed, but you *can* eliminate extra stress on your students by recognizing how demanding test taking is on young children and by making classroom choices accordingly.

Your voice quality can also help students do their best. Read test items out loud to students in a relaxed manner—even if you don't feel that way inside. Use language that is as natural as possible, while still abiding by the guidelines of the particular test you're administering. You want this experience to feel as normal as possible so your students experience as little stress as possible.

Think about pacing for those items that you read aloud to the children. For example, if a test question relates to a graph in the students' test booklets, give them a few moments to examine the graph before posing the question.

Preparing for the Mathematics

The best way to prepare your students to take a standardized test is to provide a yearlong program that emphasizes understanding mathematical concepts. If children mentally grasp the mathematics they're doing, they can often think their way through the test—much as they will have to think their way through the mathematics that come their way throughout life.

A few weeks before the test, prepare them further by giving them experiences with the new formats they're likely to encounter on the test. For instance, all year long you've presented addition and subtraction problems in a horizontal format or through story problems. Now make sure your students understand that a vertical arrangement is just another way of setting up a problem with which they are very familiar:

$$79 + 12 = \underline{\hspace{1em}} \qquad \begin{array}{r} 79 \\ +\ 12 \\ \hline \end{array}$$

This new arrangement doesn't mean they need to abandon the wonderful strategies they've developed for solving double-digit problems. But it does mean that you present them with a variety of problems, one at a time on the chalkboard or overhead, and say, "What is this problem asking you to do? How would your solve this problem?"

After students have had time to work on the problem, including sharing their thoughts with partners, spend a few moments asking them to describe their strategies to the whole class as you record their methods. For example, suppose the problem is:

$$\begin{array}{r} 64 \\ +\ 27 \\ \hline \end{array}$$

In this case, a child might say: "I know sixty and twenty are eighty. Since seven plus four is eleven, my answer would be ninety-one because eighty plus eleven is ninety one." You'll likely be pleased and maybe even surprised that, given a little time to think through this new format, your students can easily solve problems using methods that work for them.

During the test preparation period, make sure your students know how to "bubble in" the correct answer in a multiple-choice format and use scratch paper effectively. Children should also continue sharing strategies and learning from one another.

You might also take time to go over mathematical social knowledge that the students will encounter on the test. For instance, if students are likely to encounter problems involving how dollars and cents are recorded, give them some practice with these conventions. If words such as *likely* and *unlikely* appear in the test (and you haven't yet dealt with probability), introduce these terms in short lessons. For example, ponder whether it's likely or unlikely that the sun will come up in the morning, or whether the local baseball team will score one hundred runs during their next home game.

Don't do any more test preparation than you need to help your students become familiar with and confident about these new concepts and formats. Too much time spent on preparation may wear your students out and could have a negative impact on them and their test scores. Test preparation takes up valuable class time that may be better spent on other activities that foster long-term learning.

Informing Parents About Testing Issues

You have a responsibility to help your students get through standardized testing with as much support as possible. But you may also want to express your concern about any negative impact that testing puts on the children or your curriculum. Classroom teachers are often the only ones in a position to see that many standardized tests do not match the developmental stage of the age level for which they were designed. Such tests may provide little useful information to parents or teachers, or may be just plain silly in their choice of questions. Deciding whether to take what will inevitably be a political stance is a personal choice. Whatever decision you make, think through the consequences carefully.

If you do want to express concerns about testing, you might begin by informing parents. Reassure them that you are doing everything possible to prepare your students for a positive experience with the test. But if the standardized test that you have to administer affects your students in a negative way, it doesn't hurt, in a note to parents, to explain your efforts to prepare your students for the test as well as tell them of your testing concerns.

Chapter 8

May/June

MEASUREMENT AND SAYING GOODBYE

Is it really possible that the school year is almost over? We know that the passage of time happens at a steady beat, but somehow it doesn't feel that way during this time of year. There's that long, slow crawl to the winter break, followed by a quicker and steadier march through the middle of the year, and then suddenly the school year is *almost* over. And yet, it's not over. These last few weeks of school can be difficult. Everyone is tired, and you and your students may feel the anxiety that tends to creep up on humans when change is imminent.

Activities that celebrate the year in thoughtful ways can give this time a more positive feel. So this chapter reflects on the growth your students have experienced over the course of the year and explores ways to say goodbye gracefully.

The chapter's focus on measurement fits in nicely with the notion of assessing progress. The activities described below are physically active. They will give your students a chance to exercise their growing independence, with reminders that their new maturity can enable them to act responsibly. ■

Saying Goodbye

As the year draws to a close, find ways to celebrate students' accomplishments. Activities that allow children to reflect on what they've done during the year and to measure the growth they've experienced can ease the transition to the upcoming school year. Allaying fears about what lies ahead can make for a calmer, more satisfying end to the school year.

Class Yearbook

A class yearbook, to which each child contributes one page, can be a great way to look back on the year and provide each child with a memory book. A few weeks before the end of the school year, work with your students to create a list of the most meaningful activities of the year.

You might divide this list into three categories: "things we do on a daily basis," "special events," and "class trips." After the list is complete, each child can choose one topic to draw and write about. (If a topic is particularly popular, more than one child can write about it. Or, each interested party

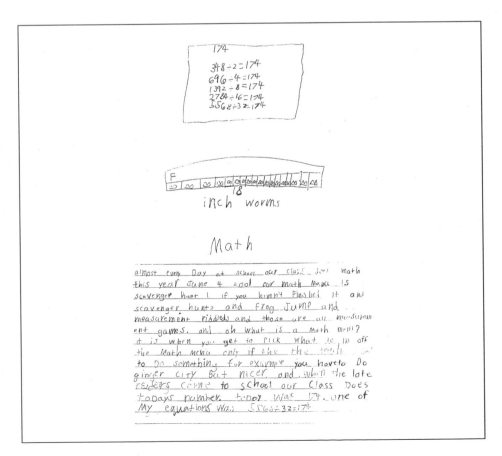

FIGURE 8–1 ◀

Jeff wrote about math.

FIGURE 8–2   ▶

Corbin enjoyed class meetings.

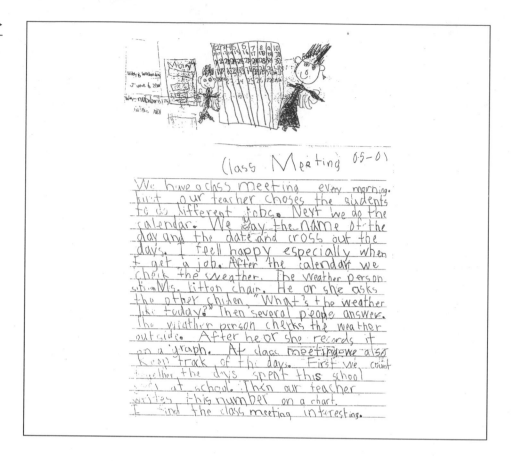

can pick a number from 1 to 10. The person who gets to write on the topic is the one who gets closest to a number that you have in mind.) (See Figures 8–1, 8–2, and 8–3.)

Compiling the yearbook might include discussing how people felt on the first day of school, for instance. Someone will likely mention how nervous he felt. That gives you a chance to talk about how normal that reaction is, and to relate feelings of nervousness to the beginning of next year. Being reminded that everything turned out fine this year may make the next transition less difficult for the children.

When all the pages are complete, put them in order of time—time of day for daily activities, calendar date for trips—and duplicate them to make a "yearbook" for each child. It's fun to pass these out on the last day of school for the children to read and color. Also, provide some time for the children to sign each other's copies of the yearbooks—a nice way for children to connect with one another on this last day.

Time Capsules

If you did the time-capsule activities mentioned in Chapter 2, refer to the artifacts you saved. The children will enjoy comparing the writing they did

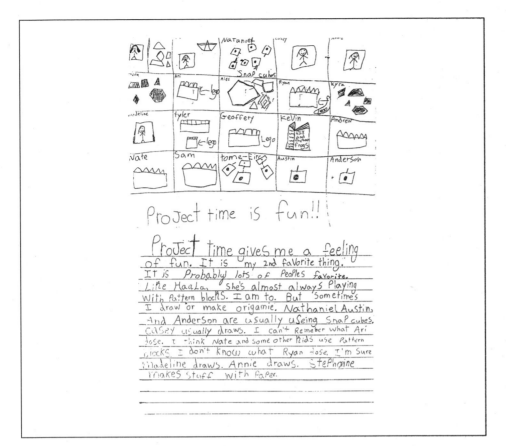

FIGURE 8–3 ◀

Ilsa took note of project time activities.

at the beginning of the year with their current work. They'll also want to measure themselves anew, to see how much taller they've grown and how much bigger their hands are now.

Reflecting on the Year: A Homework Assignment

Consider an in-class or homework assignment that asks the children to reflect on the school year. Here are some questions my colleague Lianne Morrison asks her students to write about:

"What did you like about second grade?"

"What do you wish you could have changed about second grade?"

"How have you changed since the beginning of the school year?"

"What do you hope for in third grade?"

"What worries you about third grade?"

After the children have completed the assignment, review their work to get a sense of how they are feeling. Then have a class meeting during which the children discuss these same questions.

The Learning Environment

When children are measuring, they're often up and about, moving around the room and talking to others. These conditions are a good match for the springtime needs of second graders, but they also offer children more than the usual opportunity to get off task. The operative word in this situation is *purposeful*. One way to have your students work in a purposeful way is to talk about expectations beforehand. After you've introduced an activity and before you let you students begin working, introduce the notion of being purposeful by asking:

> "What does it mean to be purposeful when you're doing a job?"
>
> "What will you need to keep in mind to do this particular job in a purposeful way?"

Talk about these issues long enough to get the sense that most of the children have internalized the importance of working quietly and staying on task. Your clues? Students offer high-quality suggestions and demonstrate a quiet and thoughtful demeanor.

Once the children begin working, they may need quiet reminders that there is still work to be done at school. Don't hesitate to stop everything and gently restate expectations if the children become overly exuberant. With the proper atmosphere established, being up and moving may be just what your students need in order to be productive—despite spring fever.

The Mathematics

Today's Number and Calendar Making

As you continue doing the *Today's Equations* activity, you'll likely be impressed that the students can write equations for numbers larger than 150! And for the calendar routine, don't forget to include a place for summer birthdays on your final calendar! Also, spend some time thinking back to the first time you asked your students to make a calendar. You'll likely be struck by how much easier it is for them to accomplish this task at this time of year.

As you turn your attention to measurement, introduce the idea that measurement involves attaching a number to length, weight, area, capacity, elapsed time, or temperature. Second graders are interested in issues of size, so measurement activities can provide numbers that capture their attention. As they measure and compare quantities, students have a chance to count and to perform numerical operations. Thus, they continue using the addition and subtraction skills they've been developing all year.

Measurement also presents some new ideas for second graders to wrestle with. These include:

- the iterative nature of measurement—When measuring length, you have to accurately count the number of times a particular unit of measure is needed to go from the beginning to the end of an object.

- ways to estimate accurately—Accurate estimating entails learning to visualize how many times a unit of measure will be needed to cover a particular distance.

- a rationale for a standard unit of measure.

- the notion that measurement is never exact—Children need to be reassured that their measurements are "close enough" because measurement is never exact.

Making Choices and Planning Time

Plan to spend several days on each of the measurement activities described below. If you're pressed for time, focus on fewer types of measurement, taking the time to do a thorough job on anything you do try to accomplish. You may want to go into great depth with one or two types of measurement—say, length and capacity—or focus on an important concept such as the need for standardized scales. See the list of additional resources at the end of this chapter for ways to extend some of the ideas outlined below.

Temperature

Temperature activities can be done concurrently with the other areas of study. After you teach students how to read a weather thermometer, add taking the temperature to your daily routine. You might want to take a reading both in the class and outside, and compare the two. Or, if your local newspaper shows temperatures in other parts of the country or world, compare your readings with those of a place in a different weather zone than your own.

Length

Stage 1: Comparison by Matching—Without Quantification

In this basic measurement activity, students match objects to a measuring device. For example, give everyone a length of string or adding-machine tape about one foot long. Students must find several objects that are about as long as the string or strip of paper and list them on a piece of paper. This simple and straightforward activity gives students a chance to work on being purposeful as they move about the room.

Stage 2: Quantification Using Nonstandard Units

Working with nonstandard units such as Unifix cubes, popsicle sticks, or paperclips gives children experience with the iterative nature of measurement. They also grasp the importance of using equal-sized units. In addition, this activity includes the important skill of estimation.

Students choose an object to measure (the length of a bookcase, the height of the chalkboard, the circumference of a trash can, etc.). They decide which unit they'll use for measuring that particular object and then record their estimate. After measuring the object using the chosen unit, they figure out how close their estimate was to the actual measurement.

"Estimate and Compare," from *Teaching Arithmetic: Lessons for Addition and Subtraction, Grades 2–3* (Tank and Zolli 2001), expands on this basic activity and provides many opportunities for second graders to compare meaningful numbers.

If your students are working purposefully on these relatively sedate activities, you might suggest some of the following things to measure and compare. (The children could measure first with string and then quantify the lengths of string with equal-sized units.)

- a one-footed hop/a two-footed jump
- a standing jump/a running jump
- two flights of a paper airplane
- the length a toy car will go on two inclined planes of different steepness
- ideas your students suggest

Stage 3: Use of Standard Units

After many experiences using nonstandard units that let them explore the iterative nature of measuring, your students may be ready to work with standard units. Introduce the idea that a standard unit of measure is useful by reading the book *How Big Is a Foot* by Rolf Myller. A perfect follow-up lesson can be found in "Body Measurements" in *Teaching Arithmetic: Lessons for Addition and Subtraction, Grades 2–3* (Tank and Zolli 2001).

After you model using inches and centimeters by measuring a few classroom objects, explain that students should now measure and record the dimensions of their own body parts: the length of a thumb, arm, foot, hand, etc.; the distance from one's waist to the floor; and so on. Partners can then compare their dimensions—always comparing inches to inches and centimeters to centimeters.

Finally, each student can compare and find the difference between his or her own body measurements and your measurements. Before you decide on the body parts you want your students to measure, think through any discomfort this assignment may cause. For instance, if you have an overweight child who will be embarrassed to reveal his or her waist measurement (or if you would just as soon keep that information to yourself!), strike that body part from the list.

Weight

You can take children through the same stages with weight that you used for length:

Stage 1: Comparison by Matching

Gather together at least twenty objects with weights up to two pounds. Ask the children to hold two of them out in front of them, noting which one feels heavier and which feels lighter. Doing this with and without blindfolds can be illuminating.

Next, place items on either side of a balance scale and note which one pushes the scale down further, to determine which is heavier. Challenge students to pick out one object and find something that is lighter than it, something that is heavier, and something that weighs about the same.

Stage 2: Quantification Using Nonstandard Units

Provide balance scales; things to weigh; and a set of objects such as ceramic tiles, metal washers, or marbles to be used as comparison weights. Children can quantify the weight of each thing by counting, say, the number of tiles it takes to balance the object. Using the data that they've gathered on several objects, they can sort the objects in order from heaviest to lightest.

To encourage thinking about the need for a standard, have students measure the same thing using first tiles and then washers as quantifiers. Ask why these two measurement tools generate different numbers. Would your student rather have ten marbles' worth of candy or ten washers' worth (assuming the washers are heavier than the marbles)?

Stage 3: Use of Standard Units

You'll need standard-sized weights (either British ounces or metric units) to use in your balance scales. You may also want to explore other types of scales, such as bathroom scales that quantify weight in standard form but use a different mechanism. Ask students, "What type of scale is best for what type of job?"

Capacity and Surface Area

Materials

- at least 1 small box—no bigger than a shoebox—for each child (ask the children to bring these in a week or so ahead of time)
- printed 1–100 charts, 1 for each child and 1 for yourself
- tiles for measuring surface area

Instructions

If you have students work in pairs, they'll have the advantage of doing each activity twice. They'll build on what they learn from measuring their first box to make more accurate predictions about their second box.

Capacity

The children will estimate the number of cubes their boxes will hold and then check their estimates by filling their boxes.

1. Model this activity by displaying a box that you have filled with cubes. Gather the children around you and, after gently shaking the box, ask for estimates based on a landmark number. For example, say, "Do you think my box holds fewer than fifty cubes, exactly fifty cubes, or more than fifty cubes?" You're developing the notion of relative magnitude. You're also introducing the idea of a true estimate, helping children avoid the pitfall of becoming overly concerned about discerning the *exact* number of cubes your box might hold.

2. After volunteers have offered their thoughts, start emptying the box, taking out ten cubes at a time. Place the cubes you've removed on a 1–100 chart to keep track of the count.

3. When the box is about half-empty, ask the children to revisit their original estimate. You might ask such questions as, "Do you think my final count will be closer to fifty or closer to one hundred?" Take care to choose numbers that work for the capacity of your box.

4. After you've modeled the activity, the children can work in pairs to first estimate the number of cubes a particular box will hold (in reference to the number 50) and then do the actual filling and counting.

5. Once they have a final count, they can color in a 1–100 chart to match the capacity of each box they measure. You might encourage partners to choose a second box that has different outside dimensions than

their first box. They can then think in terms of which box is likely to hold more and what the difference in capacity might be.

6. Once they have determined the capacity of both boxes, the children can use their numeric skills to figure out the exact difference in capacity of the two boxes.

Surface Area

Prepare for this activity by tracing around all the faces of a box on a large sheet of paper. You may want to use the same box you used to model the capacity activity above. Have a box of tiles nearby for measuring.

1. With the children gathered around you, demonstrate how you traced around one face of your box.

2. Cover one of the rectangular faces you've traced with color tiles, counting out loud as you place the tiles.

3. Now ask, "Do you think it will take fewer than a hundred, exactly a hundred, or more than a hundred tiles to cover all the faces of my box?"

4. Explain that the children will choose a box, trace all of its faces onto a piece of newsprint, and then estimate, in reference to 100, how many tiles it will take to cover their own boxes.

5. After they've recorded their estimates, the children can determine the total number of tiles needed to cover all of their faces.

Elapsed Time

Give your students a feel for how long a minute is by asking them to close their eyes as you begin to time one minute. Explain beforehand that they are to keep their eyes closed until they think one minute has elapsed. Let them know when a minute has actually passed and then spend a few moments discussing their reactions. Next, talk about how you kept track of a minute. Make sure students know how to keep track of the passage of one minute using the sweep of a stopwatch minute hand or some other method of measuring the passage of time, such as a one-minute sand timer.

Once the children know how to keep track of a minute, they can time each other to see how many times, in one minute, they can:

- write their first name.
- hop on one foot.
- draw a star.
- or do whatever task they set for themselves.

If you encourage them to estimate beforehand, the children can then compare their estimates to the actual count—or compare their output with that of a friend. (If you choose this route, think through the consequences of a competitive situation by talking about issues that are likely to come up.)

See "Integrating Measuring Projects: Sand Timers" (Lemme 2000) for one of my favorite measurement activities—an exercise that's appropriate for second graders' level of independence and responsibility at this time of year. The activity involves students making their own timers by taping together two one-half liter, clear plastic bottles—mouth to mouth. (See Figure 8–4.)

The students calibrate the timer by the amount of sand they choose to put in it and by regulating the flow of sand. You encourage them to find their own way to regulate the flow. Most will do so by reducing the size

FIGURE 8–4   ▶

Make a sand timer using plastic bottles, tape, and sand.

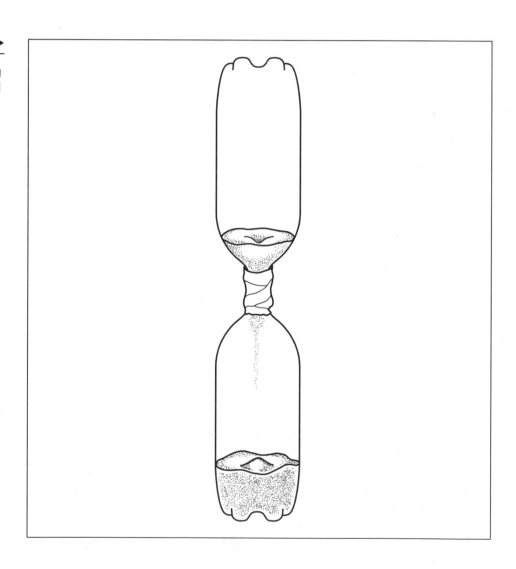

of the opening of one of the bottles using a piece of cardboard (or other material) with a hole or holes punched in it.

Demonstrate the activity by making your own sample timer as the class watches. Fill one bottle about two-thirds full of sand and then invert a second bottle over it. Have your students time how long it takes the sand to move from one bottle to the next, as you carefully invert your bottles. (It will take about ten seconds.) Discuss what might be done to make a timer that measures one minute. Don't come to any final conclusions about one right way to achieve this end. Finding the solution to this situation becomes an important part of the problem solving involved in this activity.

Making sand timers with your class requires some planning on your part. You'll need to collect enough bottles for each student to have two. (Ask students to bring them in.) You'll also need several pounds of sand. (Make sure that it's dry on the day you plan to use it.) Finally, you'll need large basins (or at least newspaper) to catch the overflow of sand that is sure to escape as the students fill and adjust their times.

This activity pays huge dividends for the children. They gain an immense sense of accomplishment, now own a timer that really works, and can go on to use it to measure how many times they (and their friends and family) can do tasks of their own choosing—in one minute!

Other Measurement Activities and Resources

The following resources can provide you with some additional measurement activities to pursue with your second graders.

Teaching Arithmetic: Lessons for Addition and Subtraction, Grades 2–3 (Tank and Zolli 2001), Measurement Comparison Lessons, Chapters 10–14

This book offers more details about some of the activities described in this chapter, and provides additional activities involving measurement of capacity and time.

Number Power, Grade 1, Boxes Unit

Don't be put off by the first-grade label attached to this book. I've used the box unit with both first and second graders and prefer it for the older children. The activities involve measuring many aspects of a box (length, capacity, and surface volume). They also provide many numeric and computational activities as well as measurement experiences. (The capacity and surface-area suggestions described in this chapter are abbreviated versions of some of the activities from this unit.) The subtitle of the series is "A Cooperative Approach to Mathematics and Social Development," so clearly it's a great resource for encouraging students to work together.

Number Power, Grade 2, Airplanes

The idea for comparing the lengths of two paper-airplane flights comes from the second-grade book in the same series. This volume also includes a multitude of activities that involve thinking about the relative magnitude of numbers—as the class makes a graph that includes data from everyone's flights and thinks about numbers within a certain range.

How Long, How Far? Investigations in Number Data, and Space Series, Second-Grade Level

This book focuses on measurement of length, beginning with direct comparison. It takes you step by step through many activities that involve using nonstandard measurement units.

Timelines and Rhythm Patterns Investigations in Number, Data, and Space Series, Second-Grade Level

This book takes children through the steps of creating various timelines. It introduces them to the concept through a year-by-year timeline of the eighty-seven-year life of Theodore Seuss Geisel (the famous Dr. Seuss, author of so many great children's picture books). The kids go on to create their own personal yearly timelines and a daily timeline for one special day from their own lives. This activity can be a nice way of reflecting on growth over time and may fit well with your end-of-year activities.

"Creating Numerical Scales for Measuring Tools," Teaching Children Mathematics (Young and O'Leary 2002)

This article describes how first graders created their own nonstandard numerical scales as they explored length, capacity, and temperature. The authors rightly claim that their students explored these areas at "a deeper level than is typical measurement activities."

Here's just a taste of what their classes did. They began their unit with a reading of Rolf Myller's *How Big Is a Foot?* This story relates the creation of a much-too-small bed for the queen. The problem occurs because the unsuspecting carpenter makes his measurements using his own small feet, rather than the king-sized feet of—who else but the king?

The students were asked, "What happens when we measure something with long footprints, then with short footprints?" Each group was given ten individual "king-size" footprints and ten individual "carpenter-size" footprints to work with. As the students measured bookcases and other objects in the room, they eventually noticed that the shorter footprints generated a larger number than the longer footprints did. However, noticing was not necessarily the same as understanding. Eventually, one student came up with the idea of measuring the same item with first the king's footprints and then the carpenter's footprints, lined up right next to the king's. This side-by-side comparison helped many of the other children finally understand the concept.

Later, the children created "rulers" by affixing the footprints to long strips of adding-machine tape. These rulers posed their own problems, because the students tended to write the numbers in the middle of each footprint, rather than at one end. For instance, an object that was actually five-and-a-half footprints long was recorded as six footprints. The students eventually solved this problem by writing the number at the toe of each print. Then they could transfer this knowledge when they created inch rulers out of one-inch pieces of tagboard affixed to a one-foot-long strip of tag.

Throughout the unit, the children were asked to come up with their own solutions to problems that arise. That's how they developed the deeper understanding suggested by the authors in their concluding remarks. This would be a terrific unit to use this time of year if you want your students to take a problem-solving approach to measurement.

Afterword

This past summer, I had a chance to experience firsthand what it's like to learn new and difficult material. My maternal grandparents were both born in Italy, and I've always wanted to capture some of my heritage by learning Italian. So my husband and I signed up to take a two-week language course in Tuscany. We prepared by taking an introductory course through a local high school's adult-education program several months before our trip. Our experiences in Italy surpassed our expectations. We enjoyed our fellow classmates; appreciated our friendly, conscientious teachers; and loved living in a beautiful village, immersed in a culture that offers everything from great food to breathtaking art. We would both go back in a minute, if we had the opportunity.

And yet, I remember feeling that I had somehow become *less* proficient in Italian at the end of the two-week course of study. During the final week of our trip, which we spent in Florence, I almost always resorted to English rather than trying to use the Italian I had struggled to learn for the previous two weeks. Here's what I think happened: In an attempt to be thorough and comprehensive, the school had devised a curriculum that presented large amounts of new material each day. The grammar class introduced a major new concept every day, and the conversation course that followed was unrelated to what had been presented in the grammar class. Review was pretty much nonexistent. There seemed to be an underlying assumption that learning would take place simply because the instructors had conveyed information clearly and in an organized fashion to attentive and motivated students.

Instead, I found myself feeling more and more overwhelmed by the amount of information coming my way. I grew disappointed in myself and the instruction, even though my teachers were kind and well meaning. I was at sea about how I could ever hope to regain my confidence and make progress. This fall, I took up Italian once again at a language school that uses different teaching methods. Instructors present new material on a frequent basis, but now it's no longer the teacher doing most of the talking. Instead, my instructor involves every student actively as we try out new learning. He encourages us to construct our own phrases, not to fill in one-word answers. We return to ideas presented in previous lessons and have a chance to use what we know of the language as we devise simple written and oral essays. I'm slowly regaining my confidence and motivation to continue learning.

This experience brought home for me the shortcomings of a curriculum that doesn't allow students the time and opportunity they need to construct understanding. I didn't go to Italy looking for thoughts about educational theory. But I came away from my learning experience with a renewed belief that, for real learning to occur, students must have a chance to *process* ideas in ways that enable them to take on meaning. I was reminded that sometimes *less* can be *more,* and that muddling around with ideas and making mistakes can lead to learning that sticks.

So, I encourage you to slow down the pace of your teaching and look at who your students are and what seems to be making sense to them. When introducing a new activity or concept, engage students in a dialogue about what you are doing. For instance, when teaching a new game, ponder aloud about your thoughts and strategies, "Umm, now, what numbers do I hope will come up?" "If I choose this five, what will I free up? Ahh—look at that. If I use the five on this side, I'll also be able to use the eight underneath it!" Encourage students to share their initial thoughts. You'll pique their interest and focus their thinking on the mathematics. Give ample wait time for students to pull their thoughts together. Accept and appreciate all attempts to participate and engage. Create a culture where learning from mistakes is seen as a positive.

Once students are working independently, support their efforts. Show interest in their thinking and respect their way of solving a problem. Value all contributions equally, but also ask questions or provide information that might lead to new understanding. Ensure that efficient strategies get shared, and don't hesitate to model ways of representing an idea through pictures, words, and other symbols. Encourage your students to help one another, and make it clear that you are there to help them learn.

Have high standards for all of your students. Let everyone attempt big problems by using strategies that make sense to each individual. Have confidence that, although solutions may vary in complexity, all children who persevere in finding solutions are engaged in meaningful work. Invite your students to stretch themselves by reflecting on what they have learned with questions that jog their thinking. For instance, ask, "Is it always true that you can change the order of numbers in an equation without changing the total?" Encourage perseverance and a love of challenge through your own willingness to try out new ideas. Laugh with your children and share your enthusiasm for learning. Second graders seem to have an innate need to like and follow their teachers' lead. When you model openness to learning, they will follow with pleasure.

Finally, don't forget you are the boss! Only you are observing your students in the classroom, so only you can decide what activities to introduce, and when to do so. That means you should take all of the ideas in this book with a grain of salt. Do what makes sense to you. Know that even if you follow the suggestions in this book to the letter, you won't have the perfect curriculum. When I look over this manuscript, I ask myself, "Hmm, I wonder where I could have fit in a unit on probability? I wish I had suggested more . . . ."

You get the picture. As teachers, we can probably never be fully satisfied that we've done all we can do for our students. This state of being keeps us on our toes—always searching for new ideas, and constantly challenging ourselves and our students in this difficult and rewarding profession.

Blackline Masters

Blank Calendar Grid
Weather Graph
Sweet 13
Odd or Even?
Pyramid 10
1 to 10
Single-Digit Addition
Adding Doubles
10-by-10 Grid for Number Puzzles
Place Value Assessment Individual Interview
Letter to Parents
Hexagon Fill-In
Geoboard Dot Paper
1–100 Chart
Patterns on the 1–100 Chart
Double-Digit Cover Up
Story Problems 1
Story Problems 2

Sunday	Monday	Tuesday	Wednesday	Thursday	Friday	Saturday

Weather Graph for _____, _____

sunny	partly cloudy	overcast	rainy	snowy

From *Second-Grade Math: A Month-to-Month Guide* by Nancy Litton. © 2003 Math Solutions Publications

Sweet 13

You need:
1 deck of cards, with face cards removed

Rules
1. Shuffle the cards, then deal seven cards to each player.

2. Leave the rest of the cards face down. This is the draw pile.

3. Player 1: Choose one of the cards in your hand, and place it face up next to the draw pile. Say the value of the card out loud.

4. Player 2: Place one of your cards next to the first one, and add its value to the first card. If the total value is more than thirteen, draw from the pile until you get a card you can play that brings the total to thirteen or less. Say the total value out loud when you're done.

5. Play continues until one player brings the total of the two face-up cards to exactly thirteen. That player sets the trick aside and gets to lead with a new card.

6. The player to get rid of all his or her cards first is the winner.

From *Second-Grade Math: A Month-to-Month Guide* by Nancy Litton. © 2003 Math Solutions Publications

Odd or Even?

You need:
    1 deck of cards, with face cards removed

Rules
Two partners will be working together, against the deck. Players might want to keep track of how many times they win and how many times the deck wins. The object of the game is to remove all the cards from play by going through the deck only one time.

1. Shuffle the cards, then take the top two cards and place them face up, side by side and slightly overlapping one another. Set the rest of the deck face down next to the two cards.

2. If the sum of the two face-up cards is an *even number*, remove them from play and turn over two more cards from the deck. If the sum is an *odd number*, take a third card from the deck and place it face up, slightly overlapping the top card.

3. If the sum of the top two cards is *now* even, remove them from play. If the sum is odd, add another card—once again slightly overlapping the three cards already face up.

4. Continue in this fashion, always looking only at the top two cards, until you have used up all the cards in the deck.

5. Make a note of who won—you or the deck!

     From *Second-Grade Math: A Month-to-Month Guide* by Nancy Litton. © 2003 Math Solutions Publications

Pyramid 10

You need:
> 1 deck of cards, with face cards removed

Rules
Two partners play against the deck. The object of the game is to pick up the
entire pyramid as you go through the deck once.

1. Shuffle the deck, and arrange twenty-one cards in a pyramid, as shown below:

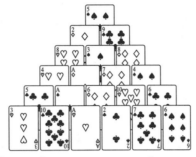

2. Put the rest of the deck face down next to the pyramid.

3. Note "free cards": A free card is one that has no other card overlapping it. When
   the game begins, only the six cards on the pyramid's bottom row qualify as
   free.

4. Remove all free 10s *and* pairs of cards that add up to ten. Set these aside. These
   cards are now completely out of play.

5. Continue removing free 10s and pairs adding up to ten until there are no more
   possibilities to be picked up.

6. Turn over one card from the deck. If it's a 10 or can combine to make ten with a
   free card from the pyramid, set these cards aside. If you *can't* use the card
   you've turned up, set it face up below the pyramid. You may be able to use it
   later.

7. Turn up another card. Follow the same instructions as in Step 6. Each time you
   are able to remove cards from the pyramid by turning over a new card, see if
   this top card is now usable with the free cards in the pyramid.

8. The game ends when you've turned over all the cards in the deck and you can't
   make and remove any more totals of ten.

1 to 10

You need:
    2 dice
    1 deck of cards, with face cards removed

Rules
The object of the game is to get rid of all your cards. One player gets all the red cards. The other gets all the black cards.

1. **Player 1:** Roll the dice and find the sum of the two numbers. Discard any set of your cards that have the same sum as the dice. For example, suppose you rolled a five and a three. That adds up to eight. You can make eight many ways: 5 + 3, or 4 + 4, or 6 + 1 + 1. Choose one way to make the sum, then discard those cards.

2. **Player 1:** If you can't make the first sum with the cards you have, roll again. If you can't make this new sum, roll again. If you can't make this third sum, you automatically lose.

3. **Players 1 and 2:** Take turns rolling the dice and discarding cards.

4. The first player to get rid of all his or her cards is the winner.

From *Second-Grade Math: A Month-to-Month Guide* by Nancy Litton. © 2003 Math Solutions Publications

Single-Digit Addition

Make sure you know your doubles. If you don't, practice them every day.

$1 + 1$ $2 + 2$ $3 + 3$ $4 + 4$ $5 + 5$ $6 + 6$ $7 + 7$ $8 + 8$ $9 + 9$ $10 + 10$

In class we looked at the chart for addition facts from $0 + 0$ through $10 + 10$. There were 121 facts! That's a lot.

When we looked at the chart closely, we discovered that there were many facts that everyone already knew, so we crossed those out.

The facts listed below are the ones that you may still need to practice. The important thing is to have strategies that make sense to you so you can quickly find the answers when you need them.

$4 + 3$	$5 + 3$	$6 + 3$	$7 + 3$	$8 + 3$	$9 + 3$
	$5 + 4$	$6 + 4$	$7 + 4$	$8 + 4$	$9 + 4$
		$6 + 5$	$7 + 5$	$8 + 5$	$9 + 5$
			$7 + 6$	$8 + 6$	$9 + 6$
				$8 + 7$	$9 + 7$
					$9 + 8$

Each day, choose three or more of these addition facts. Write your strategies for getting the answer to each fact on a separate piece of paper.

Note to parents: The purpose of this assignment is to encourage children to use their number sense (especially the ability to decompose numbers and knowledge about how numbers relate to one another) to develop strategies for efficiently doing single digit addition. Different children may come up with different strategies to solve the same problem—the important thing is for each child to think about what works for him or her.

Memorization is less important than having a quick and accurate way of coming up with the answer. For instance, when I want to answer $8 + 9$, I say, "$8 + 8 = 16$ so $8 + 9 = 17$." I can do this in the blink of an eye. In class we're talking about the kinds of strategies that make us mathematically powerful. Your child should have many ideas to draw on. You might want to share some of your own strategies with your child. Just remember that your child may go about solving the problems differently, and that's fine. We must construct understanding and methods that work for each one of us.

From *Second-Grade Math: A Month-to-Month Guide* by Nancy Litton. © 2003 Math Solutions Publications

Adding Doubles

Think of ways to represent all the doubles, from 1 + 1 = 2 to 10 + 10 = 20. For example, during the World Series there are 18 players for each game. Nine of the players are Yankees, 9 are Padres. Brainstorm ideas with your family. Use numbers, words, and pictures. Practice your doubles when you have finished. Knowing your doubles can give you strategies for adding other number combinations.

1 + 1 = 2

one chopstick plus another chopstick equals a set of chopsticks

From *Second-Grade Math: A Month-to-Month Guide* by Nancy Litton. © 2003 Math Solutions Publications

10-by-10 Grid for Number Puzzles

Place Value Assessment
Individual Interview

Name _____   Date _____

The relationship between numbers and groups of 10s and 1s
After the student has placed the twenty-four tiles into groups of ten, ask:

"How many groups of ten?" _____   "How many groups of one?" _____

Then ask, "How many are there are all together? How did you figure that out?"

The significance of the position of digits in the number
• Say, "Please leave only sixteen tiles on the table." Note how the child accomplishes this task.

• Ask the child to write *16* on a separate piece of paper. Say, "I noticed you used a one and a six to write sixteen. What does the one and the six represent in sixteen? You can show me with tiles and/or tell me."

Solving an addition problem
• Say, "If I gave you twenty-five more tiles, how would you figure out how many you had all together?"
• Write *+ 25* after the *16* that the child has written on the separate piece of paper. (Change the problem to *+ 5*, if a smaller problem seems more appropriate.)
• Note how the child accomplishes the task.
• Make sure the child knows that it's OK to write things down on his or her paper.
• Attach the child's paper to this form.

• Once the child has established that there would be forty-one tiles, ask, "If you put all forty-one of these tiles into groups of ten, how many groups of ten would you have?"

Tens _____   Would there be any left over? _____

       From *Second-Grade Math: A Month-to-Month Guide* by Nancy Litton. © 2003 Math Solutions Publications

Letter to Parents

Dear Families,

We're now in the middle of a math unit that focuses on developing understanding about our place-value system. This newsletter will give you an in-depth look at how your child is learning to add and subtract.

The way your child is doing mathematics in school likely looks somewhat different from what you remember from your own elementary-school days. Most of us learned to add and subtract using a particular algorithm (a rule or procedure for solving a problem). To add, we were taught to "carry," and to subtract we learned to "borrow." We did pages and pages of computation problems that were unrelated to any particular mathematical context. These assignments were designed primarily to help us remember the steps of the procedure that we had seen in class.

Because these methods are familiar to us, we tend to think of them as a standard for judging computational competency. Unfortunately, students frequently learn these algorithms without connecting them to the meaning of the numbers in a problem. And many adults who learned math this way are unable to figure out simple real-life problems. Algorithms were invented to streamline the process by which we compute. They are useful tools, but because they allow us to bypass understandings about place value, they are a place to end, not the place to begin.

The shortcoming inherent in our standard carrying and borrowing procedures is that they focus attention on the individual digits in the numbers rather than on the quantities that the numbers represent. Students who forget the steps of the procedure find themselves making fairly outlandish errors without even realizing they've made a mistake. And even when they do follow the procedures accurately, they often don't understand why they got a correct answer. Here are some examples of mistakes that students commonly make:

$$
\begin{array}{r} 58 \\ + 25 \\ \hline 713 \end{array}
\qquad
\begin{array}{r} 53 \\ - 16 \\ \hline 43 \end{array}
\qquad
\begin{array}{r} \overset{4}{\cancel{5}}\,\overset{}{\cancel{0}} \\ 50 \\ - 37 \\ \hline 12 \end{array}
$$

The good news is that there are many efficient ways to solve computation problems. In fact, second graders are very capable of constructing their own procedures. Suppose a problem calls for adding 58 and 25. Second graders often solve this type of problem as follows:

- Add 50 and 20 to get 70.
- Add 8 and 5 to get 13.
- Add 70 and 13 to arrive at the correct answer of 83.

From *Second-Grade Math: A Month-to-Month Guide* by Nancy Litton. © 2003 Math Solutions Publications

This method is as efficient as the "carrying" algorithm, is easy to keep track of, results in numbers that are easy to work with, and takes seconds to carry out. It is superior to the standard algorithm from a mathematical standpoint, because the problem solver never loses sight of what the digits represent. And it can be generalized to any problem.

Most of us don't know that other cultures have historically used algorithms that are different from those currently taught in U.S. schools. The following examples, from an article by Randolph A. Phillip titled "Multicultural Mathematics and Alternative Algorithms," published in the November 1996 issue of *Teaching Children Mathematics*, shows that some adults from other countries were taught the same procedure in their schools that many of our second graders devise:

An older man educated in Switzerland and a man schooled in Canada in the early 1970s both demonstrated that they had learned to add by starting from the left-most column. The man from Switzerland worked the following two problems:

$$
\begin{array}{r}
59 \\
+\ 16 \\
\hline
60 \\
15 \\
\hline
75
\end{array}
\qquad
\begin{array}{r}
481 \\
+\ 926 \\
\hline
1300 \\
100 \\
7 \\
\hline
1407
\end{array}
$$

This algorithm is one that many elementary-school children in the United States invent when encouraged to do their own thinking. That is, when asked to add multidigit numbers, most children naturally begin adding the digits with the largest place value. This is quite natural for adults as well. For example, if two friends emptied their wallets to pool their money, would they first count the $20 bills or the $1 bills?

Of course, solving the problem with the approach shown above requires knowledge of how a two-digit number is composed of a multiple of 10 and 1s, and how numbers can be taken apart and recombined. Children learn these concepts in class through games, opportunities to build mathematical models using manipulative materials, classroom discussions, and the chance to solve many problems. When faced with the task of adding two double-digit numbers together, the children use what they've learned about our number system to come up with a procedure that they understand in order to arrive at an accurate answer. Students have a profound understanding of an approach that they've constructed themselves, *and* they make many fewer errors by using it.

In the case of both addition and subtraction, it is not possible simply to tell children a procedure for doing a problem. Truly understanding what it means to combine two quantities to get a new quantity is a *mental* relationship that chil-

From Second-Grade Math: A Month-to-Month Guide by Nancy Litton. © 2003 Math Solutions Publications

dren have to forge themselves. The logical-mathematical knowledge needed to solve both addition and subtraction problems develops over time, arising out of many experiences. We need to respect and encourage children as they move through the natural stages of learning. That process can be uneven and is likely to include periods of confusion as well as learning. Children need a chance to form and reform their thinking as they develop understanding.

Students typically go through several stages when learning to add and subtract. For example, some might solve the problem above by starting at 58 and counting on 25 ones (59, 60, 61, 62, . . . 83). These students have developed an understanding of the meaning of 58 + 25. If carried out accurately, this method will give a correct solution. However, counting by 1s becomes unmanageable and is prone to errors as numbers get larger. Our goal is to help children find more efficient methods of adding and subtracting. Over time, they will learn to chunk numbers in an addition or subtraction problem so that the numbers are easier to work with. We find that students frequently develop efficiency in solving addition problems before they develop efficiency with subtraction.

The procedures that students develop in the primary grades can be applied to larger problems. When faced with a problem like 1462 + 1745 + 278, students have no need for the old carrying algorithm. Instead, they might approach the problem like this:

- 1000 + 1000 = 2000 and 400 + 700 + 200 = 1300. That brings the total so far to **3300**. (Jot that figure down to keep track of it.)
- Next calculate 60 + 40 + 70 = 170. Now the total is up to **3470**. (Jot that number down.)
- Now it's a simple matter of adding 2 + 5 + 8 = 15 to bring the total up to **3485**.

Note that it hasn't even been particularly important to line the numbers up vertically. The child has jotted down only three figures to keep track along the way. And most important, the problem solver can feel confident about the answer because he or she has remained focused on the quantities represented by the numbers, not the individual digits. Approaches like this one are efficient and accurate for solving virtually any problem we might reasonably encounter in life. You might want to try making up some hypothetical problems yourself to get a feel for how this approach works.

In the past, too many children ended up disliking mathematics and believing—wrongly—that they were not good at it. We need to turn that perception around. Mathematics is all about making sense, so we need to teach it in such a way that the sense-making is always apparent. If young children have the opportunity to build a firm foundation of *understanding* in the realm of number, they discover that they can achieve mastery over an important part of our world.

Warmly,

Hexagon Fill-In

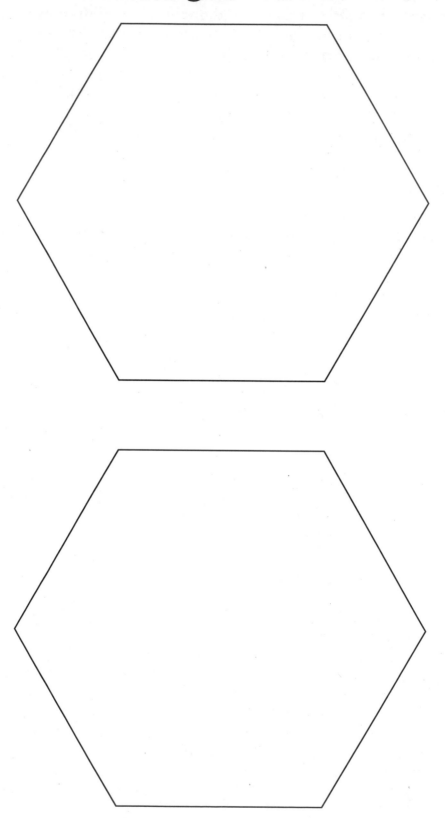

Geoboard Dot Paper

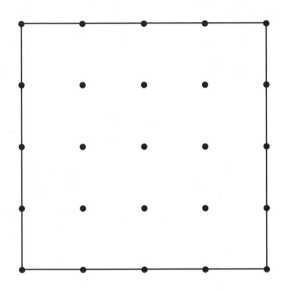

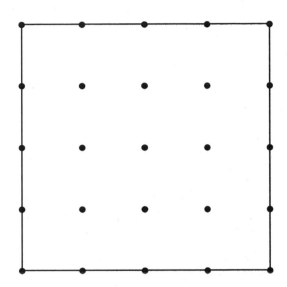

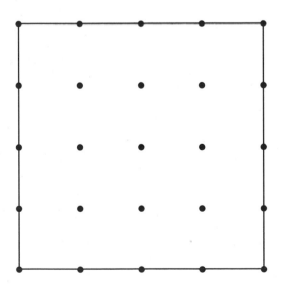

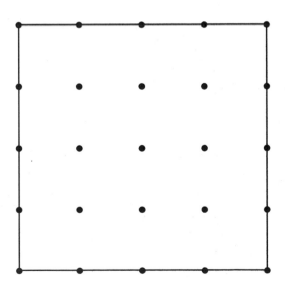

1–100 Chart

1	2	3	4	5	6	7	8	9	10
11	12	13	14	15	16	17	18	19	20
21	22	23	24	25	26	27	28	29	30
31	32	33	34	35	36	37	38	39	40
41	42	43	44	45	46	47	48	49	50
51	52	53	54	55	56	57	58	59	60
61	62	63	64	65	66	67	68	69	70
71	72	73	74	75	76	77	78	79	80
81	82	83	84	85	86	87	88	89	90
91	92	93	94	95	96	97	98	99	100

From *Second-Grade Math: A Month-to-Month Guide* by Nancy Litton. © 2003 Math Solutions Publications

Patterns on the 1–100 Chart

1	2	3	4	5	6	7	8	9	10
11	12	13	14	15	16	17	18	19	20
21	22	23	24	25	26	27	28	29	30
31	32	33	34	35	36	37	38	39	40
41	42	43	44	45	46	47	48	49	50
51	52	53	54	55	56	57	58	59	60
61	62	63	64	65	66	67	68	69	70
71	72	73	74	75	76	77	78	79	80
81	82	83	84	85	86	87	88	89	90
91	92	93	94	95	96	97	98	99	100

Double-Digit Cover Up

You need:

> 1–100 chart that has squares the same size as your cubes or blocks, 1 per person
>
> 100 interlocking cubes or blocks, some snapped into rows of 10, some singles
>
> 1 die, to share with a partner

Rules

1. Players take turns rolling the die. Players can use the same roll of the die, or each player can roll individually.

2. Each player takes as many cubes or trains of ten as the number on the die and places them on the 100 chart. (For example, if the number 3 comes up, the player may take *either* three 10s *or* three single cubes.)

3. The die is rolled exactly seven times. Players should take either 1s or 10s on each of the seven rolls. A player may not take both 1s and 10s on the same roll.

4. After seven rolls, the person who is closest to filling up the chart, without going over 100, wins.

   From *Second-Grade Math: A Month-to-Month Guide* by Nancy Litton. © 2003 Math Solutions Publications

Story Problems 1

Name: _____   Date: _____

16 + 35

Write your story problem here:

Using words, pictures, numbers, and other symbols, solve your story problem.

Story Problems 2

Name: _____   **Date:** _____

32 – 19

Write your story problem here:

Using words, pictures, numbers, and other symbols, solve your story problem.

          From *Second-Grade Math: A Month-to-Month Guide* by Nancy Litton. © 2003 Math Solutions Publications

References

Children's Literature

Bogart, Jo Ellen. 1989. *10 for Dinner.* New York: Scholastic.

Ernst, Lisa Campbell, and Lee Ernst. 1990. *The Tangram Magician.* New York: Harry N. Abrams.

Gannet, Ruth Stiles. 1948. *My Father's Dragon.* New York: Random House.

Hong, Lily Toy. 1993. *Two of Everything: A Chinese Folktale.* Morton Grove, IL: Albert Whitman.

Leuck, Laura. 1999. *My Monster Mama Loves Me So.* Illus. Mark Buehner. New York: Scholastic.

Lobel, Arnold. 1970. *Frog and Toad Are Friends.* New York: HarperCollins.

Mod, Jeanne. 1990. *The Story of Z.* Saxonville, MA: Picture Book Studio.

Myller, Rolf. 1991. *How Big Is a Foot.* New York: Dell Young Yearling.

Paul, Ann Whitford. 1996. *Eight Hands Round: A Patchwork Alphabet.* Illus. Jeanette Winter. New York: HarperTrophy.

Tompert, Ann. 1997. *Grandfather Tang's Story: A Tale Told with Tangrams.* New York: Dragonfly Books.

Professional Resources

Anderson, Catherine, Karen Economopoulos, and Alison Abrohms. 1996. *How Many Pockets? How Many Teeth?* Investigations in Number, Data, and Space Series. Cambridge, MA: TERC and Menlo Park, CA: Dale Seymour Publications.

Baratta-Lorton, Mary. 1994. *Mathematics Their Way.* Rev. ed. Menlo Park, CA: Addison-Wesley Longman.

Burk, Donna, Allyn Snider, and Paula Symonds. 1991. *Math Excursions 2.* Portsmouth, NH: Heinemann.

Burns, Marilyn. 2001. *Teaching Arithmetic: Lessons for Introducing Multiplication, Grade 3.* Sausalito, CA: Math Solutions Publications.

Chapin, Suzanne H., and Art Johnson. 2000. *Math Matters: Understanding the Math You Teach.* Sausalito, CA:

Math Solutions Publications.

Confer, Chris. 1994. *Math by All Means: Geometry, Grades 1–2*. Sausalito, CA: Math Solutions Publications.

Contestable, Julie, Shaila Regan, Carol Westrich, Susan Alldredge, and Laurel Robertson. 1995. *Number Power, Grade 2*. Menlo Park, CA: Addison-Wesley.

Cory, Beverly, and Tracey Wright. 1996. *Timelines and Rhythm Patterns: Representing Time*. Investigations in Number, Data, and Space Series. Cambridge, MA: TERC and Menlo Park, CA: Dale Seymour Publications.

Cory, Beverly, Marisabina Russo, and Joan Akers. 1996. *Shapes, Halves, and Symmetry: Geometry and Fractions*. Investigations in Number, Data, and Space Series. Cambridge, MA: TERC and Menlo Park, CA: Dale Seymour Publications.

Dacey, Linda, and Rebeka Eston. 2002. *Show and Tell: Representing and Communicating Mathematical Ideas in K–2 Classrooms*. Sausalito, CA: Math Solutions Publications.

Economopoulos, Karen. 1997. *Coins, Coupons, and Combinations: The Number System*. Investigations in Number, Data, and Space Series. Cambridge, MA: TERC and Menlo Park, CA: Dale Seymour Publications.

Fosnot, Catherine T., and Maarten Dolk. 2001. *Young Mathematicians at Work: Constructing Number Sense, Addition, and Subtraction*. Portsmouth, NH: Heinemann.

Goodrow, Anne, Beverly Cory, and Catherine Anderson. 1997. *How Long? How Far?: Measurement*. Investigations in Number, Data, and Space Series. Cambridge, MA: TERC and Menlo Park, CA: Dale Seymour Publications.

Lemme, Barbara. 2000. "Integrating Measurement Projects: Sand Timers." *Teaching Children Mathematics* 7: 132–135.

Litton, Nancy. 1998. *Getting Your Math Message Out to Parents*. Sausalito, CA: Math Solutions Publications.

Phillip, Randolph A. 1996. "Multicultural Mathematics and Alternative Algorithms." *Teaching Children Mathematics* 11: 128–133.

Robertson, Laurel, Shaila Regan, Marji Freeman, and Julie Constable. 1993. *Number Power, Grade 1*. Menlo Park, CA: Addison-Wesley.

Russell, Susan J., Karen Economopoulos, and JoAnn Wypijewski. 1997. *Putting Together and Taking Apart: Addition and Subtraction*. Investigations in Number, Data, and Space Series. Cambridge, MA: TERC and Menlo Park, CA: Dale Seymour Publications.

Russell, Susan J., Rebecca B. Corwin, Karen Economopoulos, Catherine Anderson, Beverly Cory, and Alison Abrohms. 1997. *Does It Walk, Crawl, or Swim?: Sorting & Classifying Data*. Rev. ed. Investigations in Number, Data, and Space Series. Cambridge, MA: TERC and Menlo Park, CA: Dale Seymour Publications.

Stenmark, Jean Kerr, Virginia Thompson, and Ruth Cossey. 1997. *Family Math for Young Children*. Berkeley: EQUALS, Lawrence Hall of Science, University of California.

Sullivan, Peter, and Pat Lilburn. 2002. *Good Questions for Math Teaching: Why Ask Them and What to Ask, K–6*. Sausalito, CA: Math Solutions Publications.

Tank, Bonnie. 1996. *Math by All Means: Probability, Grades 1–2*. Sausalito, CA: Math Solutions Publications.

Tank, Bonnie, and Lynne Zolli. 2001. *Teaching Arithmetic: Lessons for Addition and Subtraction, Grades 2–3*. Sausalito, CA: Math Solutions Publications.

Wickett, Maryann, and Marilyn Burns. 2002. *Teaching Arithmetic: Lessons for Introducing Place Value, Grade 2*. Sausalito, CA: Math Solutions Publications.

Young, Sharon L., and Robbin O'Leary. 2002. "Creating Numerical Scales for Measuring Tasks." *Teaching Children Mathematics* 8 (7): 400–405.

Index